P9-CFR-294

FIRE AND BLACKSTONE

FIRE AND

J. B. LIPPINCOTT COMPAN

BLACKSTONE

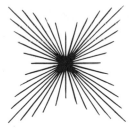

John R. Fry

PHILADELPHIA AND NEW YORK

Copyright © 1969 by John R. Fry
All rights reserved.
First Edition
Printed in the United States of America
Library of Congress Catalog Card No.: 73-91672

The passages from *Catch-22* by Joseph Heller,
copyright © 1955 by Joseph Heller, are
reprinted by permission of Simon & Schuster.

Biblical citations are from the Revised Standard Version of the Holy Bible. Copyright 1946
and 1952 by the Division of Christian Education
of the National Council of the Churches of Christ
in the United States of America.

Chapter 19, "Peace," has been published
in *Approach* and was reprinted
in *Christianity and Crisis*.

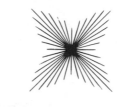

CONTENTS

Contents

PART ONE

The Background

THE BACKGROUND

I.

On being called to the First Presbyterian Church of Chicago in June of 1965, I used my first weeks in the city to have a look at the immediate parish. I walked up and down the streets and alleys of Woodlawn, talking to the citizens, just getting the feel of the place. My eyes were stunned by what was coming at me. The name of the place should be Blackstone Rangers and not Woodlawn. The children sang "Mighty, Mighty Blackstone" as they played in the streets. Graffiti on the walls of buildings, on underpasses, on street signs attested to the presence of various Blackstone Ranger clubs: Apache Rangers, Maniac Rangers, Conservative Rangers, Russian Rangers, F.B.I. Rangers, Imperial Pimps Rangers, and so on. The adult population was both fearful of, yet simultaneously unwilling to articulate this fear of, the Rangers. Groups of young men, presumably Rangers, could be seen massing in the Scott Elementary School yard in the late summer afternoons, or walking twenty or thirty in a group through the area.

In time, representatives of the Chicago Boys Club Woodlawn unit approached First Church with a request to use the church's third-floor gymnasium for a program it wanted to run with the Conservative Rangers. We granted this request. So we began to see the Rangers up close. We assigned to a member of the congregation—a student just graduated from the University of Chicago and awaiting matriculation at Union Theological Seminary in New York—the task of providing a full history of the Rangers plus an up-to-date analysis of over-all organization. The Session of the First Church received his report in January, 1966, and pondered its possible significance for two months.

One whole area of significance was right out in the open. It was becoming unsafe for man, woman, or child to be on the streets after five in the afternoon as a consequence of the fierce nightly war going on between the Rangers and their rivals, the Devil's Disciples. The high rate of violence was disruptive of elementary community life. Life was swiftly becoming intolerable in Woodlawn.

We had visions of bulldozers crouching on the edge of Woodlawn, all gassed up and ready to level the place. Woodlawn had tipped from solid white to solid black in the fifties. It was about ready to tip into nonexistence in 1965–66. People were being shot at and were shooting every night. The Chicago Police Department did not express any official public alarm over the situation. If anything, they were minimizing it. Furthermore, the apparently benevolent city agencies assigned the general task of programing for ghetto youth could not sustain relationships with the Rangers, not because the Rangers thought them too square but because they perceived them to be on the same side as or as identical with the police. In April of 1966 Woodlawn suffered the most violent single month in its history. The young men involved in some of this violence showed every sign of expanding their activities. In that same month the Session of First Church authorized the employment of two experienced people, Charles LaPaglia and Robert Keeley, to begin some kind of association with the Rangers, with the direct purpose of ameliorating recent violence. We had little idea of the consequences of that single act. No one else was doing a thing. *Something* had to be done.

May, 1966. The Southern Christian Leadership Conference had contacted the Blackstone Rangers. A meeting was planned. I consented to allowing S.C.L.C. the use of First Church's John Knox Hall for the meeting. S.C.L.C. showed a CBS kinescope of the Watts riots. The Reverend James Bevel followed with a speech in which he advocated peace between the Blackstone Rangers and the Disciples. He then outlined a program of civil disobedience calculated to bring the city of Chicago to a full halt. Mr. Bevel was more excited by his program than the four hundred Rangers who had turned out for the meeting. The numerous plain-clothes detectives present noted the nonchalant Ranger reaction but dutifully made ominous reports of the meeting. Superiors who read the reports seemed to minimize the actual Ranger reaction and to maximize the threat which a combination of S.C.L.C. and the Blackstone Rangers posed to the city. From that moment on, Chicago's officialdom was dedicated to a policy of full heat on the Blackstone Rangers.

Charles LaPaglia and Bob Keeley had been feeling out ways to start a programmatic relation with the Rangers but had scarcely gotten to know the main leaders. There was considerable use of the third floor of the building, especially the gymnasium. No defined program was yet under way. Later that month police arrested seventy-five Rangers on disorderly conduct charges arising out of a meeting of no more than *twenty* of them in a schoolyard; some of them seventy-two hours *after* the schoolyard meeting and some despite ironclad alibis, such as being at work when they were alleged to have been in the schoolyard. This event indicated the new policy. The Session voted bail bonds for all arrested Rangers who could not raise the money themselves. Thirty-seven bonds of $25 each were needed. I interceded with Judge Harry Comerford for all seventy-five.

The mere acts of providing bond and appearing in court

with the Rangers signaled to the police that First Church was involved. They were furious. They had no good words to say for us. They insisted that had we not interfered, all seventy-five would have been kept in jail, off the streets, in the critical summer months when a lot of violence was being anticipated. In several further incidents during June, First Church provided bail bonds. The Rangers began to hold dances on the third floor each weekend. Charles La-Paglia and I were generally available for discussions in my office on the second floor of the church building. Frequently Ranger leaders would meet in that beautifully appointed room, which featured parquet floors, an oriental rug, and a bank of stained-glass windows facing the east. Ranger leaders were asked to confer with U.S. Treasury Department agents and members of the Chicago Police Department for the purpose of arranging a disarmament. As a result, the Rangers did disarm to a significant extent, and all weapons not falling under Federal jurisdiction were stored in a large walk-in vault on the second floor of the church building. These weapons were carefully inventoried by the Federal and local police authorities. The combination of the safe was known to only two ladies on the church staff, mature women of impeccable character. Yet four months later these weapons were confiscated in a "raid" by policemen who pretended they were acting on secret information that guns were in the safe, at least one of the raiders having himself helped to place the weapons there.

Our third-party role in the disarmament demonstrated our desire to reduce the general firepower in the area. Ranger leaders maintained that violence reduction was their number-one concern too. In fact they explained the growth of the organization in that light. They had, so they said, originally banded together to resist the aggression of other boys and establish some basic security; they had encompassed adjacent areas for the purpose of expanding the size of the Ranger enclave—what they referred to as the "hood"; they had fought when they had to fight in order to maintain the integrity of the hood. They had grown enormously, according to them, *not* in order to inflict death and pain on others but to protect themselves. Our steady question in response to this generously mythologized story was: "If you are so strong and well organized, why can't you knock off the violence with the 'Ds'?" To which there was no answer. They would not attempt to give us unbelievable answers. They just had no answer. But the question had force and pertinence. We were not subtly but directly trying to relate the possibilities of their contemporary experience to mythologized Ranger history.

In early August the Rangers began to present themselves publicly. They picketed the War on Poverty office on August 1. On August 14 they secured a package deal from the youth welfare Establishment. Representatives from several youth-serving agencies paid for an out-of-town picnic on Bud Billiken's Day. The Rangers took the line that if they stayed in town they would have to go to the parade in force and invite combat, which they did not want. Bob Keeley arranged for the use of the stadium and adjacent facilities at Notre Dame University in South Bend, Indiana, and nine hundred Rangers spent the day away from trouble.

More and more Rangers began using the church building on a regular daily basis. We were having more than one hundred Rangers in the building at all times from early afternoon until curfew, which meant well over three hundred Rangers every day. My office became a sort of hub of Ranger activities, especially those activities involving other institutions and city agencies. And during late summer the Rangers requested use of the main nave and chancel of the church for meetings of the entire "nation." This steady and heavy use of the church irritated youth workers in regular established agencies because First Church did not and would

7

not undertake any supervision. It was our desire to place that task squarely on the shoulders of Ranger leaders.

Please understand. The Blackstone Rangers had a terrible reputation. Almost without exception Woodlawn residents hated and feared them. The organization was known to be armed and quick to use firearms and other instruments of violence. Woodlawn residents thus believed that First Church must at least be sanctioning and probably even participating in these activities. The church building had been violence free. It had suffered far less damage than other institutions which furnished their own supervision. But the apprehension grew. So I wrote a background paper in September for the congregation. This "black paper," openly critical of certain practices of the Chicago Police Department and of the policies of the youth-serving agencies, ranks next to the S.C.L.C.-sponsored meeting in importance. What had been intended as a clarifying statement designed to relieve apprehension in the First Church family ignited whole new sets of angry discussions on the South Side. The focus was not so much on the content of the paper as on its existence. The business of serving youth is a jungle. Agencies compete fiercely for the finite number of dollars available. They guard their actual programmatic intent carefully in their proposals. Behind such a performance lies the sobering possibility that no hard thought has taken place. Styles are set by simply consulting the political barometer. The gauge tells them what it is possible to do; i.e., eventually the funding sources must check with City Hall. Thus the mere existence of the black paper was a bomb. When Lieutenant Edward Buckney later testified before the McClellan committee, for instance, he entered the black paper into evidence without further comment. Its mere existence was thought sufficiently damning in itself.

Response to the black paper in the congregation was almost wholly favorable. But Woodlawn was riled up. The

Woodlawn Organization* was riled up. Even though there was a steady decrease in actual streetside violence, the case of First Church "working with" the Blackstone Rangers was being prosecuted inside the heads of citizens and First Church was being pretty consistently found guilty—not guilty of something criminal but guilty by association. Therefore in October the Session called a convocation for the church family. Its purpose was to allow full discussion of the Blackstone Ranger program. I presented a paper (see page 149). The discussion was moderated by Mr. L. D. Jones, a ruling elder in First Church and a brilliant moderator. The paper contained four theological principles meant to provide a theological resource to discussion. But discussion did not follow. Many strangers were in attendance. At least one of these was a plain-clothes policeman. Others were serving in South Side agencies. Many did not announce affiliation or name. They spoke vociferously against the program. They asked insinuating questions. Charles La-Paglia, Bob Keeley, and I sought to counter the more grossly misleading statements but without much success. Members of the congregation with real questions had no opportunity to ask them. The theological principles themselves were not discussed at all. The convocation was a bust. It had been wrecked by the filibustering of vocal, angry, and uncomprehending representatives of the youth welfare Establishment, including a policeman.

The church building was raided on November 10, 1966. Wide publicity attended the event. First Church was portrayed by police sources as the headquarters for the Blackstone Rangers, as having been used for storing weapons. This was not true, but the best efforts of the staff to present an alternate view were largely unsuccessful. Thus what had

* *The Woodlawn Organization, begun in 1961 with the aid of Saul Alinsky, has become the most significant community organization on Chicago's South Side.*

been rumored freely throughout the South Side became, because it appeared so prominently in the newspapers and on TV, a fact believed to this day by thousands of residents of metropolitan Chicago.

Members of First Church were initially enraged and be- wildered by the raid. But from that point on they began to expose their own uneasiness about the whole program and particularly the heavy use of the building. Rangers were there morning, noon, and night. They used the first floor, basement, second-floor offices, and third floor. Ordinary church meetings had to kind of wedge Rangers out of rooms in order to begin. There was writing on the walls. The kitchen was occasionally broken into. There was a lot of dirt, mud, snow, ice tracked over all the main halls, plus cigarette butts on the floor and general littering. The rest rooms were inevitably messy. Custodial service could not keep up, which was distressing to the congregation. A feel- ing began to develop, from these internal experiences of constant uproar and great numbers of Rangers and from outside allegations about First Church's being the Ranger headquarters, that the church no longer belonged to the congregation but to the Rangers instead.

Congregational feelings were muted. Still the issue did not turn into a showdown, because the dissenters recognized that First Church was in the midst of an important work. The nondissenters were ecstatic. They had never belonged to a church with so much booming activity, and no one had *ever* heard of a church that people broke into if it didn't happen to be open.

The Blackstone Rangers had been a small street-corner gang, violent, secretive, parochial, just like a hundred others in the city or in any other city. But as early as 1965 First Church had seen the Rangers break out of their form. They had developed techniques to curtail violence. On several remarkable occasions they had come into full public view and made definite public commitments; they were no mere Woodlawn organization but encompassed the entire South Side and were precisely *unlike* any other youth organization in the city. First Church's programmatic aims (as articulated in the black paper) were to reduce violence; to establish relationships between the Rangers and South Side institutions, agencies, and organizations; and to provide social, political, and economic options beyond what the South Side environment could and would provide. By speaking out repeatedly against police harassment, we became identified by the police as a source of trouble, even of criminality, and of independence at least equal to the Rangers themselves. This had the consequence of deflecting some of the official wrath away from the Rangers while their organization was developing the style and leadership patterns required by their new public position, which was helpful to the Rangers and hard on First Church.

It seemed the city was punishing us for what we considered to be the only realistic thing a Christian church could do: namely, work for peace, save life, and make war on the structure of disease. But *any* effort seemed to come under condemnation from the city, and especially the Chicago police, when we provided bail bond. This was construed as a sinister activity, although sanctioned by the Bill of Rights. When we sought to provide legal defense, and at times *adequate* legal defense, to Rangers, we were treated as though we were assaulting the judicial system itself, instead of helping it to function. When we expressed friendship for Rangers, invited them to our homes, rode in automobiles with them, sat with them in public places, and when we accepted their friendship, visited their homes, attended their weddings, or walked with them down the street, the general community was helped to believe that we had forsaken morality itself.

The rumor mill began to churn: The staff of First Church

was getting rich off the Rangers; it was getting perverse sexual thrills from the Rangers; it was providing guns, ammunition, and training to the Rangers; it was Communist; it was under the dominion of an unnamed white racist located in, of all places, Madison, Wisconsin, and as his lackeys the staff was fostering conflict between black boys as a means of population control. To the man on the street, where there was so much smoke there just had to be some fire. In such a context the report of a shooting incident alleged by the police to be "gang related" reinforced the ordinary citizen's estimation of First Church. Many church members were losing friends over this Ranger business and were spending practically all of their time at social events in heated argument. A few church members joined the opposition. The point is that the relevant theological issues were seldom discussed. The pertinent philosophical considerations were simply not entered into because the subject was apt to be "Does John Fry have a Swiss bank account?"

We survived that bitter winter of 1966–67 with hardly any funds, and those funds arriving late (and, because late, already committed twice), with real destitution (I mean *hunger* and frostbite), and with a few valiant lawyers working overtime on a huge volume of cases. We survived on the hope that spring would eventually come, bringing a lot of new possibilities. It did. The Woodlawn Organization (T.W.O.) successfully negotiated the political rapids with its Job Training Program, funded for one year at $927,000 from the demonstration grants division of the Washington Office of Economic Opportunity. It specified the employment of Blackstone Ranger and Disciple leaders as subprofessionals and provided stipends for job trainees. Although this excellent program was apparently impeded by the Gang Intelligence Unit of the Chicago Police Department and was vigorously fought by youth-serving agencies in the city, although employers refused to open technical training facilities to job trainees, and although the program has been maligned nationally, it remains the most stirring idea to have come out of the whole war on poverty.

Spring brought a $50,000 grant from the Kettering Foundation to First Church expressly to provide Blackstone Ranger leaders time and incentive to develop programs and get them funded. It was an educational grant made on the presupposition that self-determination must be identified, treasured, supported, and its fruits honored. To be sure, most of the grant money was eventually spent on lawyers and for bail bonds, but that grant had a tremendous impact on the Ranger nation. For out of the planning and education it provided came the organization of a political understanding that to this day represents the Rangers' best hope.

Spring also brought the creation and production of a musical revue called "Opportunity, Please Knock." When first announced—"The Blackstone Rangers with Oscar Brown, Jr., present . . ." the revue was discounted. But it played to S.R.O. crowds the first weekend and thereafter to large and appreciative audiences who paid the going rates to see what one professional reviewer called "the best show in town." It caught Chicago unawares. The music, staging, dancing, costuming, singing were first class. The ideology was simple and powerful. The cast and crew were paid amply each week during its six-week run. The initial debt contracted for costumes and lighting equipment was paid off. And a great many citizens were forced to make some re-evaluations of the Blackstone Rangers.

Momentum developed along with the greater hopefulness. The Rangers played a cool hand during the tense summer days when riots were going off in Newark and Detroit. They had negotiated a truce with the Disciples that was holding up. Violence in Woodlawn was down to zero.

But the Chicago police looked upon the T.W.O. program, the Kettering grant, and "Opportunity, Please Knock" as unqualified disasters because they brought money to gang members, and when gang "kids" have money they cause trouble, despite prevailing evidence that the money was having the opposite effect. So, operating on that theory, the police got cracking as soon as Labor Day had safely passed. Ranger leaders were arrested on an assortment of charges from armed robbery to rape and murder. The charges seemed to the Rangers and First Church staff to be largely frame-ups. Job Training centers were harassed, as were staff members of First Church and T.W.O. personnel. The winter of 1967–68 was hard in its own way, because our energies were drawn away from creative positive work and used up in strictly defensive actions. I would estimate that the Rangers lost their chance for five million dollars in new programs: Instead of planning they were in jail or commuting to court.

In June, 1968, it became clear to us that Senator McClellan was preparing to conduct a thorough "investigation." However, we had no idea just how sensationalist this investigation might be. Since First Church's involvement in the Job Training Program had been minimal, we assumed that we might be asked just a few questions about our participation, i.e., the terms of the lease agreement we had with T.W.O. for the use of the third floor of the church for one of the training centers. Instead we discovered that *we* were the target, or made to appear the target, in order the better to wipe out T.W.O.'s program. So there before the whole country the material which had been floating around the South Side as rumors was presented as "evidence." If any of those witnesses opposed to First Church had given their testimony without the immunity accorded them by the Senate rules, especially in a court of law, they would either have been laughed out of court or sentenced to 312 years in jail for misrepresentation. But they did have immunity. Therefore they safely made their outrageous allegations, smiling all the way. Attempts on our part to rebut were stifled. We were not allowed to cross-examine adverse witnesses and thereby show up the incredible inconsistencies and inanities, the malice and lack of substantiation that were so plain to us who were forced to listen.

That warning to the churches of the land: "Be good or we will bust you!" has not come true. First Church is not busted. It has scars, it is weaker in resources because of the enduring hostility of the Chicago Police Department, but it is still going and is unimaginably stronger for having lived through that experience.

II.

The foregoing material might lead a reader to believe that First Church had only a single program. That is what most people in Chicago believe, and most Presbyterians. They have heard only this one thing and, even if told about others, soon forget because of the exotic—bizarre—Ranger program. Well, the record should be clear. First Church does a lot of ministry besides the Blackstone Rangers. In a way, the most consistently inaccurate assertion had been that First Church is a headquarters of the Blackstone Rangers, said in such a way that any other activities would be impossible to imagine, so grim and evil are the Rangers, blah, blah, blah. Well, let's just see about that!

In the summer of 1965, as Head Start money began to flow, members of the congregation had alertly been preparing a proposal for a Head Start school at First Church. Woodlawn's need was there. The money was there. So First Church people decided the church should open a school. These decisions had been made well before I arrived in June. I joined right in. We got the summer program under way and then determined on a year-round school. Promptly we found ourselves on a bureaucratic obstacle course. We discovered the million ways devised by the city of Chicago to make a ministry difficult. While an apartment down the street might be in gross violation of the building code and an actual health and safety hazard to little children, the same code would be enforced in scrupulous and picayune detail when time came to inspect the fireproof, spacious, and indestructible First Church. And we had to comply or else the structure would not have been declared safe for these same children who *live*, down the street, in that violation-ridden building whose owner has "fixed" the inspector. We did comply and on December 1, 1965, commenced a permanent Head Start school for 100 children. Three Head Start units now exist in Woodlawn, which has a population of over 80,000. Thirty units might conceivably be adequate. It was the judgment of First Church that we *had* to open the school or sell the building and quit.

As we registered the children and became acquainted with their families, we discovered numerous instances where they had been excluded from public school. It may sound incredible but it is nonetheless a fact. Children were excluded from attending public school on a peremptory diagnosis of social immaturity, mental retardation, or brain damage. If tests verified the initial diagnosis, the children were placed on a waiting list for admission into one of the few special facilities the public school maintains. That practice has since been altered. But in 1965–66 our horror quickly turned to anger. We developed a little experimental school for some of these excluded children in the Head Start classrooms after the Head Start children had gone home. We learned that neither the peremptory nor professional assessment of the children had been accurate. They were basically normal ghetto children who spoke black English, exhibited disdain for the public school, and usually had some specific learning deficiency which was susceptible to remedy.

From preliminary experimental findings we drew up a proposal for a school for 100 of these excluded children. It was presented at precisely the historical moment (June, 1966) when Congress first cut back antipoverty funds. Although we had received oral commitments to proceed with the hiring of faculty and registration of children, and did, we learned after we had started that we would not be funded. We were out in thin air. We used our last bequest money to sustain the school while we bartered with Chicago antipoverty people. The Wieboldt Foundation made an emergency grant and literally saved us. The school was eventually funded for thirty-six children, and its operation continues. It turned out that political activity undertaken by church people in the June, 1966, election (about which I shall soon comment) had had a marked relationship to the difficulties we encountered in securing funds for this hopeful and unique educational venture.

We still seek permanent funding for the school; we are still operating on interim grants from the Wieboldt Foundation and gifts from individuals, notably Mrs. Joseph Hibben. We have discovered that over 60 per cent of the children excluded from school altogether are capable of doing grade level or better than grade level work. We have even better reason to criticize those summary diagnoses made by teachers and administrators of public schools: We have evidence that some of the children excluded as *brain damaged* have since become head of their class.

We also created a Political Action Colloquium for the purpose of doing independent political work in the Woodlawn precincts located near the church. This group decided to support the candidacy of Abner Mikva, who was running as an independent Democrat for the U.S. House of

Representatives against machine-backed Barrett O'Hara. This was a hard campaign. The Colloquium assumed the full responsibility for four precincts. Mikva lost the district, but he won in our precincts. At that time it did not seem strange that a church would be doing precinct politics, but after our encounters with the power of the machine during and after that election, our little precinct victories take on considerable novelty. We discovered at absolute first hand what will be required to beat that machine in 400-plus black South Side precincts. The cost of producing sufficient impact is staggering.

From 1959–60, First Church played a key role in initiating the procedures which led to the creation of The Woodlawn Organization. Charles Leber and Buck Blakeley were co-pastors at that time. Though they were not altogether responsible for T.W.O., it is fair to say that T.W.O. might well never have started without them. They were ardent and skilled participants. Since 1965, First Church involvement has been deepened and broadened by the Political Action Colloquium. P.A.C. task forces join in the work of all T.W.O. standing committees. P.A.C. has displayed its muscle and sense of humor at all T.W.O. meetings, from weekly steering-committee meetings through annual conventions.

While the Blackstone Ranger program was our most flamboyant ministry, it was, then, not the only thing we were doing. That the full span of our activities was known to so few people can be attributed to the malice with which officials of the city portrayed us in the news media. But that is not the main point.

The formation of a Head Start school, the Excluded Child school, an association with the Blackstone Rangers, direct precinct political organization, and new links with T.W.O. were discrete activities. No theological rationale was necessary in order to justify them. That they had to be done was enough justification. There *is* a full-blown intentionality in the act of perception, as phenomenologists claim. Well, the *point* is the whole bundle of subsequent obligations that each one of these initial obligations produced. If we were concerned for Head Start children, then we had to go on into the area of the families and their eviction notices, occasional hunger, legal troubles, and fires. If we were in association, no matter how tenuous, with the Blackstone Rangers, then if the police arrested seventy-five Rangers for nothing, we had some obligation to bail them out and follow them to court. If we were going to establish a school for excluded children, because it had to be done, and a major city agency withdrew promised funding, then we *had* to skate on the thin ice of financial disaster. Otherwise, how could the school ever hope to secure full and permanent funding? One thing leads to fourteen others. In 1964 the church building was open three days a week to save on utility bills. In 1966 a door check of the people who entered the church building during a week turned up figures like 4,500 or 5,000.

Let me hasten to add that each of these activities was perceived by the machine—that is, by City Hall, by the Establishment—as dangerous. The common denominator seen in these activities was a kind of sinister black independence. The police initially saw our association with the Blackstone Rangers as a deterrence to their ability to wipe the Rangers out. The machine saw our original precinct politics as a sort of freak success, though probably ominous. Then, with T.W.O. expressing organizational concern for the major youth organizations in the area and writing job training proposals, First Church began receiving a more consistently harsh treatment from the Establishment. Once T.W.O. took the line that "these are our children and we must care for them," the authorship for that concern was assigned to First Church. And to each new provocation we were forced to respond or get out of business completely. Our response tended to inspire fresh provocation, until finally First Church faced a U.S. Senate investigating subcommittee before nationwide TV. This in turn has obligated us to respond in a way that will certainly further enrage the Establishment.

Some of the abstract and romantic talk about "ministry in the world" makes it appear as a set of one-shot surgically clean actions. You go do your ministry, then you relax and rest up, apparently, before doing another ministry. This is a bemusing whimsey. "Ministry in the world" means being literally terrified that the telephone will ring just one more time and someone on the other end will be needing something you probably don't have but will find, some way or another. "Ministry in the world" is, in fact, a disgusting expression which should be banished from further use. There is no such thing. First Church did no "ministry in the world." We joined Woodlawn.

III.

Well, this is not a history of First Church. This is a book of sermons which occurred during that history. I preached the sermons. As I read through them, my memories of Union Theological Seminary flood in on me. I reminisce. About George Buttrick and Paul Scherer during those halcyon days, so long before Woodlawn. 1950.

Buttrick and Scherer were two great preachers who had been gobbled up from their great churches and installed into the Union system of a great faculty for its perpetually great student body. These two great preachers taught their students to preach great sermons. They *were* great preachers. Theologically top flight. Imaginative. Tough. Rhetoricians of the first rank. Their casual conversation was more polished than most people's formal written prose.

So members of the great Union student body would

come to preaching class with assigned sermon outlines. George Buttrick taught a course in sermon outlines. Introduction, three points, conclusion. The student would write his outline on the board. Buttrick would exclaim at its novelty, scriptural soundness, and general cohesion. The effect of his estimate was thrilling. Student thought he had unwittingly committed a Masterpiece. Therefore, said Buttrick, let us make it super-great. The preacher-teacher then would suggest perhaps a minor reordering of the points so that the realignment might read three, one, then two. This suggestion was made in the interest, of course, of achieving yet clearer expression. Not squarer, clearer. Finally, Buttrick would offer a suggestion for the introduction, brand new, from his own overflowing originality, plus a new conclusion, based on all the new and realigned material. There. The student outliner learned how to do great outlining.

Paul Scherer believed in outlines right next to Jesus. The points of an outline are to a sermon what the backbone is to the body, he would say. The outline should shine out of the sermon. Everybody who hears a sermon should be able to tell you your structure in your own words when the sermon is over. Scherer himself preached what he considered to be outline sermons. Although of the one thousand listeners he would preach to, you could not get any five who could say what the outline was. And *he* was right. The outline was there, shining out of the sermon. His hearers were dense. But what good is an outline shining out of something, if the something is not itself super-shining—brilliant? He was a prose man, first, last, and always. His sermons were written in sharp prose. He knew the sound of greatness. He would not settle for less from his students. In his preaching classes a student would occasionally present a pretty good sermon. When that happened Scherer might respond with real salty tears of exaltation. That was seldom. Mostly he was muttering and making nervous little asides and laughing in a nonfunny way as a student sermon was being presented. Scherer's creativity was, you see, reconstructing the whole bulk of what he was hearing into a first-class sermon. By the time the student had finished, somehow Scherer had not only heard and remembered every word; he had also thought of better, more felicitous, more striking words, and less crude ways to say them. He would illustrate. Now, when Paul Scherer said "Good morning," it was high-quality stuff. When his adrenalin was up, he was the unsurpassed world heavyweight talker champion. He would resay the student's words into great words, which, *off the cuff*, were suitable for binding into any book of great sermons . . . to the astonishment of the entire class.

Great preaching. Brilliant, penetrating, clear prose, delivered in smooth tasteful ways, from the diaphragm, through relaxed vocal chords, then mixed, stopped, and shaped by efficient tongue-tip–teeth-ridge articulation. And scriptural, morally passionate. Theologically gifted. Union was turning out a preaching elite for those great churches in the land still interested in great, nonpedestrian, nonpietist, exciting, and illustrious preaching.

I look back to those days, 1950 and thereabouts, in much the same way and with much the same wonder as I look to the seventeenth or the second centuries: interesting days that have gone by, full of their own contents but definitely not for this day. Great preaching is just no longer appropriate. For the principal reason that there are so few great churches in which the great preaching can be done. The classical great sermon in a less than, or no longer, great church is worse than inappropriate. It is an anachronism. An irrelevance. Like a Lyceum lecture at a go-go palace or a Klan rally. I mean, one of those beautiful sermons—three points, amply and aptly illustrated, solid, and Biblical, constructed in style suitable for sending to *Harper's* on Monday morning—these sermons have got to have beautiful churches full of people who might discreetly note a minor syntactical lapse. And that is the kind of church we are fresh out of. The presence of national issues has forced a reconsideration of the whole matter of greatness. A big church which makes a mighty witness is great by the *new* terms of greatness, as is the little church which hangs in there, even if a spider now and again can be discerned crawling around on a pew. The new terms of greatness come from action in response to these issues, not because of brilliant preaching. In fact, great preaching—in that fine old three-solid-points-and-lots-of-stories tradition—to a white-power bunch becomes anti-great, as well as grotesque. Aspiring to great preaching in that same white-power situation is ridiculous. The greater the words, the more greatly they mock preacher and hearers alike if they do not well up from within a situation of action.

Add to that reality another mark of the difference between this and an earlier time. Rhetoric, even brilliant rhetoric of the highest quality, is heard to be the equivalent of political and commercial rhetoric and is thus heard to be either a subtle pitch or bombast. The flashier the pulpit performance, the more likely the preacher is to be considered a conman. *Unless* he tailors his rhetoric to the pre-set sermonic expectations of the bunch he is preaching to. Then his rhetoric is not brilliant; it is sold out. Imagine Paul Scherer or George Buttrick in their prime, preaching to some well-groomed segs out there in two-car land somewhere. Bow! Zap! Crunch! the words would say. The listeners would yawn, daydream, or otherwise endure, having already overcome. The very style of the preaching, no less than the Biblical contents, would signal the audience to turn off all receiving apparatus.

Fire and Blackstone

The time for great preaching of great sermons to great churches is over. I knew this to be a certified true fact before I was called to be pastor of the First Presbyterian Church of Chicago, which had had in its long history more than its rightful share of great preachers. This church is a charter member of the no-longer-great church club. The congregation no longer fills the 1,200-seat nave as it once did. It no longer attracts swell people with their swell money. Although the church building has diminished none in size or formidability, the neighborhood has quietly slipped into slumness. The parking lot, half a block away, has a bent gate and broken glass all over it because it has become the play place for maybe a hundred neighborhood children on a regular basis, one of whose regular delights is smashing bottles on the asphalt. Whoever heard of a great church with broken glass on its parking lot or with empty wine bottles heaved into its shrubbery? Well, whoever heard of a great church in a slum at all? That is the main question. There is a direct proportionate relationship between the declining membership of First Church and the almost 100 per cent black population in Woodlawn. The swell people took off. And they took off primarily because black people had begun to join the church. And when more and more black people joined, as more and more segs took off, the ratio leveled off at fifty-fifty. That congregation, once 2,400 white folks now become 500 black and white, is simply a no-longer-great church. The question in 1965 was whether or not the transracial congregation could survive the rigors of confrontation with ardent black power and the erosion of white membership by shock and death. That was the question when I came in 1965.

We were thinking positive thoughts, of course. Like becoming great again. We were thinking of augmenting the membership, building up a new financial potential, watching over the happy racial ratio, and putting on some attractive programs calculated to advertise how gloriously multiracial and transcultural we really were. It was fine planning, showing excellent forethought. Except history did not allow us to get to our agenda. History has not provided the time to reachieve greatness. Had we stuck to the agenda, the South Side probably would be in ashes and Woodlawn demolished, including an apostate First Church.

Do not think this is inverted boastfulness, to wit: that First Church is a great church but in a different way. We certainly are not. We presently have a membership of 585 which is somehow raising an $85,000 annual budget. This is the basic and first and necessary $85,000. Because we have it, we receive about $420,000 a year from other sources. The people of First Church realize that this extra money from the government, foundations, and individuals will not always be available. But the ministries we have inaugurated will not be any less worth doing just because money is not available. So we *must* build ourselves up to an annual basic budget of $500,000 just to maintain what we have going now. Go ahead. Do the basic arithmetic. Something like 3,600 members, all giving at the fantastic levels of the present near-600, would be required. There is plenty of good reason to want to grow and to become great. There is solid basis, besides the fear of pain, for the universal desire among First Church people to have the time and freedom from harassment required for growth.

But such time and freedom do not happen to have arrived yet. As I write this we do not know what new charges, indignities, threats, and assassinations of character await us, or, for that matter, what new ministries we shall have to undertake. Perhaps we shall die as a church, by attrition, because our resources have had to be expended at a rate faster than the rate at which they come in, with little time at any time to secure new resources. It has been the boast of Daley lieutenants that the machine can beat down any dissidence successfully because it can wear any organization down in so many ways. To the question of a possibly newly great church, at least in Chicago, must be annexed the alternate question of a possibly dead church.

The recent history of First Church has not allowed much time for the consideration of preaching, either, except that once a week the congregation gathered, the order of worship said "Sermon" right after the New Testament lection, and so there was a sermon. Without considering the matter at all, it was just obvious that "great" preaching (introduction, points one, two, three, with lots of stories, then a conclusion) would not do. After three and one-half years I am amazed that I took so little thought for the impossibility of preaching to that congregation. I mean: A.D.C. mothers and their children, Ph.D's, professional people, nonprofessional people, of both races and different ages, theological students, college students, the socially conservative (to the right of bloody Marys) and socially liberal (to the left of marijuana), Republicans (a few), Democrats, the new left, anarchists, radical black-power people, occasional Blackstone Rangers, policemen, lifelong Presbyterians, lifelong nothings, former Baptists, former Methodists, former Lutherans, former Congregationalists, Jews, Catholics, and not a few fiercely anti-ecclesiastical friends of First Church. Had any thought been given to that spread of people, the preacher would have been immobilized.

Well, happily, a new age of preaching has dawned which sees—properly, I think—that the life of the congregation validates preaching and not the other way around. Here is what I mean: We came to church one Sunday morning and found that (official?) vandals had entered the church building sometime Saturday evening, turned on the hot- and cold-water spigots for a mop sink on the third floor, and the water had flooded the third floor, the steps and hallway of the second and first floors, and dripped through many electrical fixtures into second- and first-floor offices and classrooms. So a squad of worshipers took off their shoes and swabbed the place out while the service was going on. At times plain-clothes police with not inconspicuous guns have been right there in the back pews. For many weeks the lighting apparatus for a full-blown musical revue was in the chancel and nave. A polished third-draft sermon in that scene would be wildly incongruous as well as impossible.

There has been no time to consider reflectively the problem of preaching. Typically a thirteen- or fourteen-page handwritten sermon manuscript was prepared on Saturday night. Sometimes the entire Saturday night. This meant that the selection of a Biblical text, done sometime earlier in the week, was all that had been done. Exegesis, thought, theological work, preparation, and writing had to be telescoped into simultaneous operations. Which is another way of saying that the preparation of sermons appears on a continuum with the preparation of proposals and running over with $25 to the local police station to bond out some Ranger chief. Preaching, in short, was forced to be flat out because that was the style of the church.

There is considerable variety in the sermon sample collected here. It reflects the variety of issues, concerns, and problems indigenous to the congregation. A heterogeneous congregation shows this variety. I believe that First Church people are unanimous in their desire for full self-determination by black people of black people. There unanimity stops. Certainly no consensus could be developed on art, politics, the war, the Bible, or air pollution. Nothing close to general agreement is possible on worship, church music, black power, or Ornette Coleman. The glory of the congregation is the tolerance which holds such a heterogeneous group together. This tolerance allows for the strong, forthright statement. Not even but *especially* in the pulpit. The pastor is, after all, only one man. He does not speak for, he speaks to, the congregation. He speaks his own mind as clearly as he can. Thereby he invites criticism as well as bemused disagreement. All that is required is that personal statements not be marked down because they are personal. The congregation knows. When the preacher says, "The Biblical point of view is . . ." he means, "I understand the Biblical point of view to be. . . ." Personal statement is automatically adjusted for. Allowances are made for overstatement, or error, or excessive passion—gladly made, because personal statement is so much more appropriate than general fairness and objectivity. People can hear fairness and objectivity all of the time, every time, in fact, they read the newspaper or look at the ten o'clock news. What do fairness and objectivity turn out to be? Inevitably favorable to the Establishment. During the Democratic Convention in Chicago in August, 1968, the local press started out reporting the news of what was going on in the streets from the standpoint of a lot of reporters and photographers who had been banged on the head. The press was angry. But then it began to realize, not that there was *another* side, namely, that the police were keeping the convention safe from Communist agitators, but that the press was against Mayor Daley's line. So they hurried onto that line and somehow repressed the (vivid) memories of having themselves been beaten. "But in fairness it must be remembered," the commentators would say, "that the police were subjected to abuse and obscene taunts." Objectivity prevailed. What happened to one-thousand-plus people beaten and gassed badly enough to require medical attention? Objectivity wiped them out. The Mayor called them Communist agitators, and what is good enough for the Mayor is good enough for Chicago.

In our congregational study of Frantz Fanon's *The Wretched of the Earth* I recall enthusiastic approval and excited discussion of Fanon's description of the objective reporters covering the Algerian War. These reporters were always snooping around trying to get both sides of the story, and writing the French side with the Algerian side as a foil. Well, as a church we had been living through the both-sides-of-the-story experience with the local press. Our side was never actually presented. The other side always was. Objectivity is tilted. That is why personal statement has been welcome in the First Church pulpit. Personal statement does not mean "our side gets said on Sunday morning." Personal statement means more than favorable, automatic, propagandistic discharge. Personal statement is a display of active thought, intended to rally the active thought of the hearers.

The regular appearance of Biblical material in these sermons deserves some comment. In a kind of traditional, pooped-out, Protestant way the Bible should be the source, content, and occasion for *any* and *all* preaching: Great Preaching Revisited, or the Son of Great Preaching. Why the Bible "should" be is found in what Protestants always do. Rank, funky Protestantism is showed up right there in that blessed "should." The Bible then is made to live up to all the expectations buried in the "should." It becomes what it is expected to be. Slavishly the preacher says, especially on Reformation Sunday, "For freedom Christ has set you free; do not submit to any new bondage." And no one laughs.

The Bible is a fantastic book. It has these great stories. A perfectly amazing point of view, once it emerges out of the goo and iron bars and hymns and candles. It is against civilization. Money. Religion. Greed. War. Demons. Disease. Death. Poverty. Greed. Propaganda. Injustice. Sin. Lies. Idiocy (political). Repression. *Reader's Digest*. The Bible believes in God, in Jesus, in the Holy Spirit, in the church. The holy people. Joy. Forgiveness. Love. Life. Justice. Peace. Truth. Passion. Ecstasy. Health. Prosperity. Affluence. Resurrection. Without going some Barthian old way and fawning around over a lot of *dead* Christian thinkers, including Augustine, Luther, and Calvin and what *they* said about the Bible, on its own terms it is simply a fantastic, marvelous, rich book. If the American Establishment had any idea what was in that book, it would be hunting Bible readers and forgetting about lunatic Communists. It is so much more than infallible, or holy. It is . . . radical. And flat out. You put your hand to that plow, slip the thing into drive, and hang on. You can't look back because of the acceleration. The text wants to go so much farther than the preacher ever expects, and gets to some astonishing places. The reading of the lections *is* the high point of the week, if for no other reason than, and for the perfectly glorious reason, that it is going to be revealing. Thus attention replaces conventional adoration.

The sermons in this volume are arranged in an order suggested by some public nonsermonic utterances made to the congregation and to various other collections of people across the country. These papers develop and analyze materials in a rather more formal way than the sermons do. The sermon sample is representative. It contains neither the best nor the worst, neither the most nor the least egghead, neither the funniest nor the saddest sermons. It does represent what was typically happening during the time marked off for sermon on Sunday mornings. The speed with which the sermons were prepared shines through, and this fact is reciprocally related to the speed with which everything else happened and had to be done. But on reading them now I have no desire to straighten them up into first-class great sermons, even if I could. The only additions made are the titles, and these were inserted by the publisher. After all, who would read sermons without titles? But that's the point. Titles are for great preachers. Great sermons always have great titles posted Monday morning on great lawns in front of great churches. Well, if you don't have a sermon until Saturday late you can't post a title on Monday. And if you don't even have a lawn . . . why have titles? The titles in this volume, then, are our only compromise with greatness, and as you can see by their brevity we were not willing to go very far.

A final word. This collection would never have happened without unremitting harassment practiced on me by members of the Political Action Colloquium, and especially John Fish. They have fancied a connection between action and sermon and claim to perceive a correlation between the style of the preacher and the style of the Colloquium. Quite apart from this, since the Colloquium is going to get the royalties, they are interested in money with which to conduct campaigns. The Reverend Mr. Fish deserves special mention. He is the leading harasser. He is a participant in the Colloquium, through recent years the administrator of the Doctor of the Ministry program at the Divinity School of the University of Chicago, and a procrastinating finisher of his Ph.D. thesis on The Woodlawn Organization. He has overcome my morbid cynicism about sermon collections with straight power. He says, for instance, "Well, look at it this way. These are not sermons at all. They have no titles. They are all much too long. They contain no illustrations, no stories, no poems. They are really nonsermons." Moreover, he and fellows in the Colloquium have done all of the work, except preparing this introduction. I suppose I should thank them for all the trouble they have gone to, but I cannot muster up the words. Even a book of nonsermons is an excrescence on the publishing industry.

What I do thank them for is the hope they continue to nourish that Richard J. Daley can be defeated in 1971. Because they have such a hope and stand so fiercely for independent, creative, black, self-determining politics in the four hundred black precincts of the South Side, their desire for this book can be tolerated.

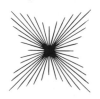

PART TWO

The Breakdown of Democracy in Woodlawn

1

THE BREAKDOWN
OF DEMOCRACY
IN WOODLAWN

Democracy, to the citizen, is a series of streetside operations which have symbolic characteristics. The policeman
and the courts present the citizen with a wide gamut of
operations, in some of which he may be directly involved.
He may be a traffic-law violator; he may seek a divorce.
His children may be helped across a busy street on their
way to school by a policeman. The whole set of operations he sees and hears about have, beyond their empirical
meanings, this additional *symbolic* characteristic. Simply
as phenomena, and altogether as a set, these operations
symbolize law and order. Democracy is really charging
on when the police and the courts engender respect for
law and order, when, as Peter Berger once noted, there is
installed inside each citizen's head a metaphysical cop. A
democracy presupposes law-abiding citizens.

In the same way, the school system—public and private—

---

*Following the police raid on the church (November 10, 1966)
and the ensuing publicity, I spoke to various groups in the city
and suburbs. This address, "The Breakdown of Democracy in
Woodlawn," was delivered on several occasions in late fall, 1966.*

35

is for the child a dreary sort of thing he has got to do. Empirically, the school is something he has got to get up for, go to, endure while there, and escape with relief from each day. It really isn't that bad, but he likes to put us on that way. The reason he keeps going is that he is forced to by the democracy. There is a law about this matter. Moreover, Mommy and Daddy believe in school ever so passionately, believe in doing well, in trying hard, in moving ahead. The school is seen by the parents not merely as a remedy for the general stupidity of children but also as the training event for entry into the economic apparatus of the country. That is its symbolic characteristic: it promises to turn out educated people who can function economically, politically, and socially—but basically economically. Democracy is on the march when the children grow up, have children of their own, and begin sending *them* to school because the children-grown-up-to-be-parents believe in school as a set of empirical operations and as a symbol of the country's need for alert, aggressive, intelligent, i.e., educated, citizens.

Now the polling place is another operation that has contents of an immediate nature and also a symbolic characteristic. The citizen has a vote. It is sought by candidates and their parties. The citizen evaluates these direct bids for his vote and then, with his fellows, casts his vote. All of the votes are counted. The candidate with the most votes wins. Through such a procedure the citizen is helped to see that he is the real boss in a democracy. He chooses his representatives. His voice is determinative for public policy. And he believes what he is helped to see: namely, this symbolic characteristic. The polling place is where he casts empirical, countable votes but also is a shrine of democracy itself. A democracy really going somewhere has got citizens who earnestly believe the symbolic characteristics, who make informed political judgments, and who, therefore, participate deeply in this democratic experience.

Last: the home. The home is people living together and has all of the daily stuff of that shared life. It is the place where the Bill of Rights, the Constitution, its preamble, the Declaration of Independence, the Bible, and other central doctrinal sources come true. For the home is far more than mere protection from the wind and a ready source of nutriment. The home is the deluxe ethos-radiating institution in the whole democracy. The home makes clear the symbolic characteristics of the other democratic institutions. The home teaches the young to want to become good participants in school—and the economic order. The home teaches the young to respect law and order. The home teaches the young the power of the polling place and by its very existence as a home teaches the young that the democratic dream daily comes true: namely, that dream of an abundant, productive, fruitful, and moderately happy life for all. Symbolically, the home is the bastion of democracy. And a democracy is doing fine when the young grow up, marry, and promptly establish homes of their own.

This is all very simplistic. I am being, I suppose, almost rude to rehearse these rudimentary and nonsophisticated materials for you. I appreciate your forbearance. I have lined up these materials in order to describe for you what happens when and as democracy breaks down. Not any old democracy, but democracy as a finite set of streetside operations carrying symbolic characteristics. Not in any old indiscriminate place, but in Woodlawn on the South Side of Chicago, and in all the other deep and mid ghettos of metropolitan U.S.A. where the colored poor live.

There are perceivable policemen in Woodlawn who are perceived not as friends but as enemies because of what they do. A boy growing up in Woodlawn this last sum-

mer might have been picked up for walking down the
street, given his choice of a beating or being arrested on
a disorderly conduct charge, jailed, tried, fined, and/or
imprisoned for a month or so. He takes the beating in a
dark alley and stumbles on. This boy sees a wide spectrum
of crime on the streets where he lives, and the criminals
are not promptly thrown in jail. They seem to be protected
by the police. If the boy happens by certain special places
at certain special times he can observe the payoff. He
sees whores, pimps, pushers, dealers in illicit liquor, the
numbers game operators, the policy wheel operators, all
of the functioning members of syndicated crime being
upheld, their hand strengthened. He sees, also, people totally
innocent of criminal acts being searched, beaten, taken to
the station, and often found guilty by the courts. He sees
apartments violently entered without search warrants. He
sees his fellows shot—and killed—without one policeman
lifting a finger to arrest the assailant. On occasion he may
see his fellows being shot at—and occasionally killed—by
the police themselves. Which says nothing about verbal
harassment, badgering, hectoring by patrolmen of this boy
growing up in Woodlawn.

Democracy has plainly broken down when the police
are perceived to be enemies. The set of streetside operations reveals a negative symbolic characteristic. The police
symbolize protection of the crooks. That is the law: the
crooked go free. And the police symbolize order: the order
is that any violent conflict in the community will be quelled
by the direct use of violent force. So that violence fate-
fully begets violence and that is a negative order. There
is no metaphysical cop inside this young man's head. There
is no so-called respect for law and order. He has been
taught by his own eyes to distrust—to despise—the upholders
and enforcers of the law and thus the law itself.

Now in the schools of Woodlawn streetside violence is
moderated, but violence exists there, too, mainly among

students but often by teacher initiative. The physical environment of the school is incredibly depressing. And so are the teachers and the student body. Hardly anybody believes it will work. Both the school authorities and the boy believe that he will never make it into the land of comfort and plenty. They conspire between themselves to tolerate each other until the boy can be successfully pushed out of school or he can successfully drop out. Most boys in Woodlawn, including many in high school this minute, read at about the third-grade level, which is to say they can read the *Tribune* without difficulty, read summonses, read bail bond slips, read eviction notices. They can write their names, and letters from jail. They have been prepared to function in the economy, all right, as the runaway fathers of children whose mothers survive by virtue of A.D.C.

Democracy has broken down. The schools are terrible. They inspire no hope, are not credible as educational facilities. But that is not the point. The point is that the schools have a negative symbolic characteristic. They are seen to perform punitive functions. They tolerate and often practice active cruelty. The parents do not posit hope in the schools. The children find none. So it is a busted democratic institution. Its energies are negatively oriented toward yet further breakdown.

The polling place. The polling place has a flag somewhere out in front, because the law tells the judges to get it up and flying. And at about the same time the flag begins to fly, so does the precinct captain. He gets out the vote. By "the vote" I mean all of the people who the precinct captain feels certain will vote his way. And to ensure certainty he conducts his periodic day-long wars on poverty. I mean he buys votes. He gives money, and since the bars are closed on election day, he shows his thoughtfulness by indicating where pints of wine may be found. A boy growing up in Woodlawn knows in detail the mechanics of victory at the polling place. He knows that Woodlawn citizens have no direct voice in the selection of candidates to vote for and no way to beat the machine when it really wants to win. He thus has a certain curiosity about politics, but it is the same curiosity he exhibits about the intricacies of other arcane arts. The polling place symbolizes the power of the machine to buy elections. That is a mute testimony to the breakdown of democracy. A Woodlawn boy believes as sun-clear truth that the people do not, have not, and cannot elect their representatives. The people are not represented.

Now the home is more often than not a place of violence to the Woodlawn boy, and not a haven from the terror of the outside world. The fiercely punitive and violent techniques for solving conflicts on the street are practiced in the home as well, and behind closed doors, and with full community sanction. The abscesses of ghetto life are finally lanced in the home. Here is where the American dream, just because it comes true in white America, turns into a horrifying nightmare in the ghetto. Thanksgiving at home. The food is soda pop, potato chips, bologna, if that. If the boy comes home. Christmas at home. Better spent on the streets. The less said the better. Just don't talk about Christmas. Don't mention that it is Christmas, and maybe it will go away and does. But, you see, these are fixtures on the democratic agenda. And their regular appearance reinforces the boy's belief that the home is a place to escape from because he might then escape these nauseating national holidays. The home bears a negative symbolic characteristic, just like the police, the schools, and the polling place.

The Woodlawn boy is never free from violence, terror, chaos, helpless poverty, and banality. There is no safe place in his world. He lives in an upside-down democracy, really an antidemocracy. His life chances are to end up (a) dead,

(b) in the pen, (c) a winehead, (d) a junkie. And the forces in this antidemocracy conspire to make these life chances continually available to him.

It is in terms of the breakdown of democracy that I want to talk a moment about the Blackstone Rangers, about whom I presume even residents of Lake Forest have heard. The Blackstone Rangers are an organization of very poor boys who have grown up in Woodlawn mostly, but also very poor boys who live all over the South and West Sides. Their answer to the chaos and violence and banality of life in an antidemocracy has been to create a large organization capable of producing some genuine order and some safety from this exceedingly hostile environment. With a kind of instinct for preservation they have perceived that unless they do something about their lives they will be forced to live out their life chances in nonproductive and finally destructive ways. They have done something: organized. Since they conceive this Blackstone Rangers to be their only chance and all they possess, they have organized well, even brilliantly. And while they have in their notorious past prosecuted a violent shooting war with a rival organization, the one primary purpose of the Ranger organization has been to maintain its organizational cohesion. With surprising sophistication, the leaders of this organization have surveyed definite policy options in the cold light of Ranger self-interest and have thereby come more and more to forego violent strategies and violent techniques in favor of policies that better serve the organization's self-interest. They have begun to act like a public force of major proportions that is capable of responsible and mature responses to the provocations of a misunderstanding and hysterical community. They treasure their opportunities more each day, and the more they treasure their opportunities the cooler and more decisive they become. Yet the more determined and cool they become, the more uncomprehending becomes the community—the more frightened becomes the community, and angry. All of a sudden the community has begun to believe in democracy. All of a sudden there is clamoring for these young gangsters to straighten up and get a job, to quit this silly and violent gang. "Don't you know that shooting people is wrong? That hitting, knifing, clubbing people is wrong?" They say this to boys who have nothing else to believe in and who in spite of all odds have been the first Woodlawn force to cool off the community. Now just how can these irrational and incongruous and inaccurate cries be credited, especially when they issue from the so-called Commission on Youth Welfare, from Red Feather organizations dedicated all these years so wistfully to the so-called servicing of the young? They cannot in fact be credited. They are hysterical and out of date. Badly out of date, and worse, out of focus. They do not admit the effective antiriot measures of the Blackstone Rangers last July, for instance. What is forgotten so conveniently is that the Rangers *saved* Woodlawn.

Well, I suppose it is one of these ironies of history we are always reading about, but the Blackstone Rangers, so villified for their violent ways, the organization created in the bowels of antidemocracy, has successfully raised the issue of law and order for the whole city of Chicago. And this is how. On October 11 the police began a severe effort to break up the Rangers. They arrested about fifty Rangers on that night, acting in a fiercely and cruelly provocative manner, seeking to provoke violent response from the Rangers that would give the police, in turn, occasion to react. And following that date on numberless occasions they have arrested Rangers on fantastically whimsical and incredible charges, have beaten them, have held them incommunicado, harassed, threatened . . . *bullied* the Rangers. But to no avail. The Rangers would not be provoked.

The Breakdown of Democracy in Woodlawn

They were cool. So a final effort was made. On November 10, the First Presbyterian Church itself was raided, the Ranger home. The raid was conducted in order to secure weapons that the police themselves had helped to place in a large and impregnable vault. It was trumped up from the start. A flying wedge of patrolmen stormed this bastion of calculated nonviolence with weapons drawn, safeties off; they destroyed property wantonly and needlessly. And, yes, they got the weapons that had been placed in the vault and paraded the weapons before the press and TV like heroes, painting the church to be a haven of criminals. Well, that is the way it is in an antidemocracy. The criminals daily go free and the one institution in Woodlawn that has succeeded in drastically reducing streetside violence, the one institution in Woodlawn that has succeeded in creating safety for a significant number of Woodlawn boys, that institution is raided and crucified in the press. But, as I have said, the Rangers were cool. One hundred and twenty-seven were in the church that night, playing ball and meeting with agency representatives about jobs and housing. They were searched, a few were cuffed, all were held by swaggering, verbally nasty policemen with carbines and magnum pistols at the ready. For almost two hours, these 127 boys suffered the invasion of what they have come to consider some kind of haven from violence. Without one word of rebuttal, one violent response. They maintained their fabulous cool, and when the police finally left the gym where they were being detained at gun point, they together shouted "Blackstone!" That cry was the beginning of the answer, and the full answer will be made in a court of law in which the complaints of the church of illegal police procedure, the complaints of the Rangers of illegal police procedure, will be added to complaints of citizens all over Woodlawn of illegal police procedure, so that the whole city will be let in on what has been happening in Woodlawn, and the whole city will be forced to see whether democracy is a viable political form any more. For, mind you, if the police are not checked in Woodlawn and forced *by law* to uphold and defend the law, so that citizens begin to *believe* in democracy, then the police have a free ride in Woodlawn and in other communities, and eventually, yes, in lovely Lake Forest.

The reconstruction of the positive meaning of law and order in Woodlawn could be the beginning of efforts to pour positive content into the other democratic institutions as well—the schools, the home, and the polling place. Is it not strange that the young men who have suffered most from the breakdown of democracy should now play so decisive a role in its reconstruction?

2

BLINDNESS

ISAIAH 40: 1–8   MARK 10:46–52

Please ask no up-to-date questions of the great account of the deliverance of Bartimaeus from his blindness, which is not an up-to-date account. Do not say, "Was it a disease of the eye? Did Jesus do the first corneal transplant? Was Bartimaeus psychosomatically blind, perchance, his physical blindness caused by emotional illness?" These are smart questions, all right, but the wrong questions, and questions the Mark account provides no answers for. Instead, try to stand down nineteen centuries to another world view held by another people in another land. Listen to the story the way the story was told.

Jericho was a walled city. On a main road of Palestine. Bartimaeus seated himself outside the gate of the city in order to present himself in his afflicted condition to the numerous people using the road, hence coming into or just leaving the city. He depended on pennies from travelers. Pitiful pennies. Pennies dropped because of pity. And he advertised his blindness by wailing. Poor blind man whose every day was spent in arousing token gifts from travelers. The people of the city, of course, who knew him, his history, his father, his family, did not pity him because they saw him every day and, as the residents of the city know, he could get around pretty well. He had memorized the streets, knew where to turn, could find his way. In the classic way of people who every day rub up against evil conditions, the citizens of Jericho ceased to care, to be horrified by blindness. He could die of hunger and they would accuse him of lack of initiative.

So there sat Bartimaeus, just outside the city, begging from travelers, wailing out, "Help the blind man." He sat with the other derelicts, the other beggars. Now, Bartimaeus had heard that the great healer was in Jericho and hoped that Jesus would come on the road out of Jericho because he would at least make a good hit on Jesus. Popular figure. Popular figures and candidates, then as now, are not able to afford to pass up beggars. They tend to have to perform generously. When, according to his estimation, the noise he heard just inside the city kept coming nearer him, and he got it confirmed by the nonblind derelicts that it was in fact Jesus, Bartimaeus set up a super-wailing. A tremendous racket. "Jesus, Son of David, have mercy on me!" Over and over again. At the top of his lungs. Over the wailing of the other beggars. Over the noise of the people around Jesus. Clear, unmistakably louder and more hearable than the noise. This was an impertinent wailing. Uppity. A breach of the unspoken contract between beggars and beggees: namely, that beggars be demure, their face to the ground, not overdoing it, otherwise beggees will be offended, stick their noses in the air and put their camels in low, and take off. So when Bartimaeus began his super-wailing, there were lots of people who started to shush him up. His fellow beggars, directly, and all of Israel, indirectly, who demand that beggars remain who they are and stay in the charity position, which is on their knees, quietly moaning. To all of these efforts to shush him up, to get him to remember who he was, for goodness' sake, Bartimaeus yelled louder, "Son of David, have mercy on me!" So what happened?

Bartimaeus' bad tactics worked. Jesus did hear this one piercing voice over the general loud noise. Jesus instantly understood, as any Jew would, this breach of the charity situation. And maybe for a minute was stunned by that whole scene. These human wrecks. The legless, the diseased, the blind, absolutely depending for their very lives on the whimsical pennies of travelers because the people inside the city were too callous, too used to the obvious human suffering to care for them. The charity game. These misfits and maladepts, these wrecks having to prostrate themselves with quiet wailing before travelers in order merely and barely to survive. Thus half in anger he stopped and asked a disciple to produce the man. The bad tactic had worked. The beggars next to him told Bartimaeus the people were coming after him. He threw off his burnoose and met them half way, with the dignity of the blind walking unassisted across well-known territory. Their one remaining dignity. Pay attention to this blind man as he rises up and walks toward the people coming after him. Across ground he has never seen, among voices coming from people he has never seen, under a sun he has never seen, outside a city he has never seen; he has since birth lived a private history. He has had to depend on others to tell him what has happened. He has had to depend on their eyes and yet has come to believe that these on whom he is dependent have not told him all that they see, but rather what they want him to know. If he depends on them alone, his view of the outside world, of life itself, will be warped, screened, censored, half a world, and that half the crazy half. Those who aid the blind tend to believe the blind are somehow also stupid since they accept any story. By his wits he has lived, by his sharpened wits. He would have to believe the world full of the hardhearted and the condescending. A true hustler, who, had he not been an expert, could not have survived. As he picks his way so carefully, with such exaggerated

47

dignity, he represents all of the derelicts of the earth, turned into hustlers by the hard hearts of their fellows; and more, he represents all who cannot see, who live on the piecemeal reports of others, so biased, so screened, and distorted, and as such live in private worlds instead of public worlds. He represents all who have blocked vision. They cannot see into things, or into people, or into the meaning of events. He becomes many people in those dramatic steps.

The blind Bartimaeus represented what the prophets called blindness, which had nothing to do with the physiological condition of the eyes but was, much more profoundly, a refusal to see, a stubbornness when it came to seeing. Blindness was hard eyes, evil eyes, which saw right through the plight of the poor as though they suddenly were invisible, which saw a representative of God as a troublemaker who should be killed. The blind Bartimaeus was blindness itself coming toward Jesus. He stopped. In those seconds it had taken him to come before Jesus, the entire human situation had been excavated, revealing the shape of charity, the dereliction in being blind and a beggar, and the blindness of everyone standing there watching Bartimaeus. So this representative from the side of blindness met this representative from the side of deliverance. Jesus did *not* first ask him how long he had been blind. Jesus did *not* reach into his purse and extract an especially large gift, which is the very thing he might have done. He instead asked simply, "What do you want me to do for you?" Bartimaeus could not see Jesus, his eyes. But Bartimaeus had grown skilled in listening to voice inflections. He heard no money in the voice, no condescension, no charity. So Bartimaeus lifted up the heaviest words in his vocabulary, trembling with the strain of hoping. The big super-wailer suddenly could do no more than mumble. He had no experience in hoping. He had never said these words to himself, much less out loud and to anyone. But out they came: "Teacher, let me receive my sight." Once said there was no waiting, no dramatic period when Jesus evaluated them, evaluated his worthiness. As soon said, it was done. With a mighty rush from the side of deliverance, the words were spoken with the laughter of pure ecstasy, as Bartimaeus began his laughing with ecstasy, his running around, and shouting, and jumping up into the air, not being able to believe that he could see. He looked, and pointed, and peered, and reveled in color, shapes, gradations, the slants, the roughs, his eyes trying to exhaust the infinite novelty of the total landscape, seeing more in ten seconds than most seeing people see in a lifetime.

And so a great and mighty deliverance took place outside the city of Jericho, which had consigned Bartimaeus to everlasting blindness. Please do not single out this one deliverance. It fits within a pattern of accounts. Jesus had delivered people from insanity, paralysis, leprosy, suppurating wounds, deformity, and muteness. Each act of deliverance was symbolic because it demonstrated his sad cry for the plight of all permanently hopeless people in Palestine, and like bolts of lightning these acts of deliverance illuminated the ugliness of man to man. And these mighty acts of deliverance reveal the divine repugnance with the way things are. Every deliverance at the same time a judgment on the hard hearts of Israel. Every deliverance at the same time an excavation of Israel. Every deliverance at the same time an excavation of the human plight.

This Jesus, this King Jesus, this Lord Jesus, this Jesus Christ whose name we use to adorn our prayers, was a mighty man. His might lay in being able to see the textures of misery that everyone else passed right over. The miracle was that he looked across a beggar and was stunned into outrage at the sight, while the rest of mankind passed over such sights or began searching around for a suitably small coin to give the man—if, of course, he was clever in begging for it.

It is in just such a context we ought to read the commission report on civil disorders. It highlights more than all else the inability of America to conceive, even, the plight of the urban poor. America cannot see the charity situation for what it is. The situation of police brutality for what it is. The story of the deliverance of Bartimaeus should be required reading before you read the commission report. Then you have background to understand its insistence that there is a fundamental blindness in the land. Not merely an unwillingness but an inability to see the rank disparity in the living situations of the poor to the rich. Especially the black poor. All that can be said about the plight of Bartimaeus can be transferred exactly and said exactly of the members of the Welfare Tenants Unions who spoke with such eloquence yesterday as they testified before Illinois Lawmakers down in Springfield. They talked about the enforced patterns and degradation built into our charity system.

These derelicts were accepted by Jesus, therefore, as models of the deeper misery which afflicts mankind; in the instance of Bartimaeus, the deeper blindness. Our deeper blindness: an affliction of the spirit, some deformity of affection, some crippled courage, hidden agonies, all of them, hidden behind our flashing eyes and brilliant talk. But I hope you have understood, all along, this description of blindness can go very far toward describing the fundamental blindness of all those who do not see the plight of the actually blind and who invent these charity situations. Blindness is fundamentally reciprocal.

Forever seeking Jesus in the religious places and then missing him and his mighty deliverance. Seeking him among the crosses and candles. Not there. On the road with Bartimaeus, and if we cry hard enough and assault him with sufficient impertinence there, and these great blindnesses of ours are brought before him and we are actually delivered from their clutching power. Then be prepared to meet him at this communion table. Amen.

3

DOUBLE TALK

Romans 7

Out of what private agony Paul wrote this portion of his letter to Roman Christians, we do not know. Clearly, his private agony was not important. He said, "I do not understand my own actions. For I do not do what I want, but I do the very thing I hate. . . . I can will what is right, but I cannot do it. For I do not do the good I want, but the evil I do not want is what I do." He did not mean, thereby, to expose himself as a freak. Rather, he expected that his readers would nod their heads in agreement, saying within themselves, "Yes, that is just the way it is." Paul really thought that the situation he found existing within himself was a universal situation—the way it is with all human beings.

I am not going to address myself to the entire scripture reading. Not this Sunday. Another Sunday, soon. Today I want to rivet attention on Paul's description of the two wills within man. Because this strange and strangely true word has an unusual relationship to education in America today, to education in Chicago's Fourteenth District, and, yes, to the church school of First Church.

Today a child in Woodlawn who has a lot of raw natural

ability has a better chance of being accepted at Harvard, Stanford, M.I.T., or any of the other top ten colleges in the nation than a child of equal ability living in Evanston, Skokie, La Grange, or Winnetka. This holds true only if the Woodlawn child wants to go to Harvard and directs his efforts toward that goal from kindergarten on. If that is the case, if he really wants Harvard, the Chicago school system will get him there. And he needn't have a dime. Now your regular Woodlawn child does not sit around on the curb just before he matriculates in kindergarten pondering whether or not he will go to Harvard. Neither do his parents decide for him and thereafter continue deciding throughout his school career that he is going to the best college. The Woodlawn child belongs to that tremendous brotherhood of free spirits who believe that going to school at all—kindergarten, fourth grade, or Harvard—is a direct assault on their liberty. They hate school, they say. Devoted as they are to play, to good times, to the happy camaraderie of their buddies, to bubble gum, to daytime television, school appears as a prison into which they are hurled, not an opportunity-house-deluxe in which they will find their future greatness.

Meanwhile, back at Evanston, La Grange, Winnetka, and Skokie, the child entering kindergarten—no less committed, heart and soul, to the childhood kingdom of play—finds that kindergarten is not merely a prison but a serious prison. He finds that his parents are very much concerned about his schooling. That his teachers are. That some of the finkier fellow students are very concerned. Some of them know how to read and write before they start kindergarten. So he had better start to learn, and quick. So he is aimed at Harvard from the start, whether he likes it or not, while his Woodlawn counterpart, who does not know where Harvard is and, if he did, would dislike it merely because it is a school—like Wadsworth or Tesla—does not aim at Harvard, putters his way through the first three grades without really learning to read and write, and thus almost surely wipes out the best chance he ever had to find that pot of gold under the rainbow. He may never know that he had that chance to get a Harvard degree and a Ph.D. of his choice. When he gets to ninth grade, still not knowing how to read or write, not really, he may begin to think of dropping out altogether and enjoying life, while his Winnetka counterpart is studying feverishly every night, bitten as he is by the Harvard bug, studying weekends, memorizing, reading, looking up, figuring out, absorbing knowledge like a sponge.

Before we rush downtown with our "Superintendent Willis must go" signs, I think we must think this matter through very carefully and instruct ourselves as to the nature of education and the place of education in American life.

We know that Woodlawn elementary schools make some halfhearted gestures in the direction of educational excellence. But we also know that these gestures are overbalanced by the physical facilities in which the education is supposed to take place. A Scott School classroom is not exactly inspiring. Neither are teachers who feel helpless and have given up hope. One such teacher told me recently what it means to attempt to teach children who have utterly no interest in being taught, who take books home after school, drop them for the first game, never pick them up, and then come late to school the next morning. On the whole these schools are training grounds for dropouts. It is conceivable that the best teachers working with very small classes (less than twenty) might be able to overcome some of the inertia, but that is not an automatic certainty. Even very small classes of less than twenty must be populated with children who have some developed interest in learning. Even the very best teacher is still the teacher and not the pupil. The teacher may inspire desire, try to inflame it, do all sorts of cunning things, but in the end the desire must be in the child and the teacher cannot, alas, substitute her own desire for the lack of desire in the class. This is called the problem of motivation. A motivated child is a child who wants, who positively wills, to learn. He will consequently work against obstacles in order to learn. He has this thing inside him, like a goal or a purpose, that he is going to achieve. No matter where it came from, it is there. He is motivated. But that child next to him staring out of the window is not motivated. So, watch yourselves, he must, say the authorities, be motivated. Let's find some way to pump some desire in him, give him some goals, instill some purposes, set him on fire, get him steamed up. You can only know how ridiculous this procedure is from the standpoint of the apparently unmotivated child. Here he is as he is. It has never occurred to him that he is insufficiently motivated. He dislikes school largely because he likes to play. But the authorities—teachers, counselor, principal, at times parents, ministers, policemen, firemen, mayor, politicians—all tell him it is wrong to dislike school: "You must like school. Go ahead. *Start liking school!* You *have* to learn how to read. Everybody has to know how to read. It is *fun* to read. You *can* read books." Big deal. He is trying to keep away from reading books. He really is motivated to resist reading books. But the authorities presume in the most abstract, square sort of way that reading *books* is somehow transparently wonderful. Maybe none of the important people in his life read books. Maybe all of this Dick and Sally and Puff and Spot stuff put him off. Maybe if that is what books are about he doesn't want any more of them.

Now, friends, if you are determined to use your "Willis must go" signs, I suggest that you picket on *the* issue. And the central issue concerns this baloney about motivation, concerns the almost silly assumption that a pep talk will produce pep, when everyone knows that a pep talk produces resentment and ill will.

This takes none of the legitimacy and urgency away from

Double Talk

the immediate controversy over Hyde Park High School. This does not remove one ounce of pressure from the authentic force that is building up over the autocratic and eventually preferential policies of the superintendent of Chicago's schools.

I am suggesting, however, that there is a deeper problem here that we as a congregation must be aware of. The deeper problem is double talk about education. We want to say first of all that education is good in itself. It is good to know, simply to know. It is better to know than not to know, whether you are talking about ancient history or how to play canasta. It is good to study, to reflect, to read. In itself this is a preferred plus activity. We want to say this first because we don't want to be thought crass materialists. And if we speak the truth we would have to say, first, that education is good to get you a good job. What is education good for? Cadillacs, airplane trips to San Francisco, $150 suits, your own sailboat, steaks, all the ice cream you can eat, no more snow shoveling, tickets to all the Bears games, big apartment with no rats, horse races, admiration from everyone. This is really how we Americans basically regard education. It is the passport into the land of comfort and plenty. Education is so highly esteemed because the educated man can vault over whole classes, out of the social basement into the upper middle class. Education unlocks the great doors. Go through high school and you will be always sweating a job out. Go through college and do well and take the right subjects, and you just sit there. The recruiters will come to you with, "Well, son, let's say $8,000 annual salary to start with, pension plan, retirement benefits, incentive bonuses," just to enter the training program. We adults all know this is true. But in front of the young we pretend we never heard of the facts of life. We pretend that pure scholarship, the thirst for knowledge, study for its own sake, is what education is all

55

about. The double talk is the point. In Evanston and Skokie you can get away with double talk. You can say education, better citizen, bigger inside, pure knowledge, thirst for learning, and get away with it because the child there can see with his eyes that you mean Cadillacs, $150 suits, steak, twelve-year-old whiskey, airplane trips to Bermuda, and so on. But the double talk is simply devastating in Woodlawn because the child here has no way of knowing what you are talking about. He does not see Cadillacs, $150 suits, lots of ice cream, clean streets. He does not know where Bermuda is. He does not know that this is what Harvard *means*. And so he is not motivated to go to Harvard. Harvard is just reading, only study, and not getting ahead. Because he thinks Harvard is Dick and Sally and those other fay cats.

I am ashamed to be proposing this, but I will. Be honest. If you want to, as you say, motivate children to learn to read and write and get in the fast track, do not mention the love of learning, talk only of Cadillacs, speedboats, private $1,000 pool tables, and things like that that they can understand. They are greedy little grubbers just like we are.

This is the deeper problem. We are not honest and hence are ineffective motivators. We say learning but mean money.

And the reason is that we are ashamed of having to put it this way. We are secretly ashamed of our tradition and of our performance. Here we are, a moderately well-educated congregation. Well, how much reading do *we* do that doesn't have to be done? In the line of our work, I mean. Just plain reading because the book is interesting? How much time in terms of minutes is spent in pure reflection over the course of a week? How much independent study are we capable of? Do we have time for? This is what we are ashamed of and try to cover up with our double talk. We feign allegiance to an ideal we have jilted. Even the very best of us. So the ideal is burnished the more brightly before our confused children.

I presume that this is not new material to any of you. I

presume that you have thought your way through these wasted places before. I hope, at least, that you see the urgency and the deeper problem. Because I want now to turn directly to our response as a congregation to the job.

First off, we must admit to ourselves that we are more likely a part of the problem and not a part of the cure. I mean we belong unfortunately to the best of adult motivators who are trying to overcome the wills of the young by substituting our wills for theirs. We act as though the deeper wisdom of Paul were unheard of here. We act as though we were never children or had children of our own to lead us back into the mysterious regions of childhood and the child's positive dread of books, pencils, crayons, and the paraphernalia of school. To that extent we talk *at* the child. Make him do things he is unwilling to do. But we do not thus overcome him. We merely force him to put us on his list of uncomprehending authorities. We thereby become a part of his problem. In order to become his colleague, ally, friend, servant, helper, we must see how authentic his natural resistance to education is. We can do this best by acknowledging that we ourselves have never quite gotten over our own resistance. That there is a willfulness deeper than our bright surface talk against the new, the incomprehensible, the startling. We also resist hard work, unless, of course, it promises to yield cash.

So to the children of Woodlawn, to the children of our congregation, we belong to you in this human situation, on your side against motivators, bright helpers, would-be friends, and we shall demonstrate this solidarity with you by insisting that they speak true words to you and no more double talk.

Second, we have to maintain among ourselves some rather constant understanding that being comes before having, buying, using; that being is more complex than having, buying, using. Hence we can afford to honor no one because he has, has bought, uses, consumes. Among us no one is better than the next because he has been to college, maybe Harvard, maybe not. Among us no one is better than the next *period*. We have this private position on the human ladder. Now this is not a verbal witness. This is a lived witness—one that can be felt.

Not only does such a witness create giant waves of relief among all concerned at no longer having to carry unnatural designations, at no longer having to deceive and make believe. It also gives us the only possible platform left in America to insist on the integrity of education that is not aimed at a diploma and prestige job; namely, the integrity of education as such.

So that is the kind of education we should work for in our public schools and the kind of education we do among ourselves. Shortly we shall have a weekday school, and we have a regular Sunday church school and are planning some adult education that might grow to be a very important part of our over-all education program. In all of these activities we can display a gentle commitment to words because that is what human beings use to talk with, and it is important for human beings to talk expressively and intelligibly. We can display an equally gentle commitment to facts—not to fantasy, half facts, propaganda, ideology, or worn-out facts, but to the immediate actual way things are. Especially when we deal with the Bible and traditional materials of the Christian faith, we can be stubbornly insistent that no particular view receives disdain or automatic rejection. When children are late, do not attend, fly airplanes, punch each other when they do arrive, we take it as an eloquent expression of disinterest and take it seriously; do not punish it, talk to it, inspire guilt over it.

If we must insist, then let us insist always that whoever does attend any educational activity is treated for exactly what he is. We do not, for instance, have a Sunday church school because the children are the congregation of tomorrow. (This is not true; consider mobility patterns in

America's population.) They are here-and-now children, and the church school is in their behalf right now and right here. Not tomorrow. And we can maintain a gentle pervasive commitment not to learning but to the human being learning; we thus honor the human being that has been graced and dignified by Jesus Christ's presence as a human being. We honor the human being who slowly, carefully, perilously wanders all around a possible insight. And we watch, hopefully. Then he takes it for his own. With luminous surprise, he says, "Yes, I see." For those moments when human beings actually learn we have arranged an educational program and pin nothing on it, immediately. For this and this alone do we have education. The deeper and more persistent our dedication to education as such, the more believable we become in a general culture which believes in education merely as a gimmick useful in hustling cash.

We end where we began: Paul's picture of the double will. The immediate will we know, and contemporary educational theorists know and professional Christian educators know. This is the will which says, "I am going to do thus and so this afternoon," which must on occasion acquiesce to a stronger power. This is the will which wills the good and does not do it, that seems to be unable to help itself in doing the evil. But Paul pictures a deeper will, committed to more enduring goals, profoundly stubborn, untouched by ordinary experience and untouched by ordinary education. This is the core self from which springs man's true grandeur and his profound misery. It is a realistic picture. Therefore let us do no more reaching around, trying to adjust human beings and their wills. It could be that gentle respect might be precisely the occasion whereby the deep and possibly destructive stubbornness in us all is overcome and we begin thus to will and occasionally to do the good. Amen.

4

ARROGANCE

Amos 7:10–17

With the exception of the reading you heard moments ago, the book of Amos is a collection of his prophetic oracles. What you did hear is the account of the prophet's confrontation with the king's priest, Amaziah. This Amos, who did not even have any credentials as a proper city dweller, this rural type from the sticks, came to town and delivered

---

This sermon was delivered two days before the 1966 primary election in which the House of Representatives seat in the Second Congressional District was hotly contested. Abner Mikva, an independent Democrat, was running against Barrett O'Hara, an octogenarian and the regular party—machine—candidate.

The Political Action Colloquium of the church was spearheading the campaign for Mikva in Woodlawn on the grounds that the people needed a congressman who would be responsive to the people of Woodlawn. Despite the Colloquium's success in the precincts around the church, the power of the machine again prevailed in Woodlawn and Mikva lost by a narrow margin.

Two years later Mikva ran for Congress on the regular machine ticket and won. The Colloquium and a good many Woodlawn voters sat out that campaign, failing to see how they could vote for any of the national or local candidates.

the Word of the Lord. He then met Amaziah in a show-down sort of confrontation. That amazing scene, which actually happened, will occupy us all morning.

Before Amaziah called Amos he first met with the king, a man named Jeroboam who had no talent at all for being king. A real jet-set king who was the admired leader of the super-big-consumer, Jeroboam could not take time away from his snorkeling, surfing, partying, flying to Acapulco in his private jet, visiting and being visited by others of the idle rich—he could not take time away from this to be king. So the king's adviser ran the country. And we know imme-diately what that meant. Immediately the business of Israel was business. The Chamber of Commerce was saying things like free enterprise—Moses led the people of Israel to this new land so that we could control the interest rates—and other similarly stirring patriotic utterances. We also know that the law-enforcement agencies were dedicated to up-holding the sort of law and order which aided the ongoing business of Israel: namely, business. A plausible case can be made for this course of action, you know. If business is hurt, it moves away. There go your taxes. There go the responsible people in the community: Leaders, they are called. And we also know, almost by inspection, that the country will have an unimaginative foreign policy because the policy is made up by career diplomats, career army officers, and career clerks with career pencils which can only write that the situation is stable. It is the nature of career diplomacy to report what it thinks wants to be heard and not what is happening.

We know all of this as soon as Amaziah catches the king one morning before polo. Amaziah was the priest of the king's chapel. Chaplain to the king. And, as is not in the least remarkable, a very powerful man in a nation as osten-sibly religious and as practically heathen as Israel. He *did* have the king's ear. Because when he told Jeroboam all of the hateful, mean things Amos had been saying about the administration, Jeroboam, late to polo, said, "Whatever you say." A trusting king, you see, who had found that if you can't trust a preacher—well, there is not much left to trust, is there? Amaziah had the king's ear, and he had the king in his pocket. Who was the real king of Israel? The king's chaplain; Amaziah could therefore put a robe on any cut-throat operation, and apparently did.

Armed now with the explicit sanction of the king, Amaziah had Amos rounded up and brought to him. Let us pay some particular attention to the actual reported words that Amaziah spoke to Amos: "O seer," he began, trying immediately to put Amos down: seer, not a regular priest properly educated, ordained, and *trained;* not even a regular prophet who had been to prophet's school and knew the proper place and function of a prophet. "O seer"—O weirdo, O witch doctor, O fortuneteller. Amaziah was trying to do two things at once. He was trying to impress Amos with the true power of the king's priest and to intimidate Amos. (You might write that down in your notebooks: when you meet the Man, he will first try to show you his superiority and then to threaten you into believing his message.) "O seer," Amaziah began, "go, flee away to the land of Judah . . . eat bread there, and prophesy there." Notice he did not ask Amos to shut down his message directly. Not in so many words. Not right out in the open. Instead he told Amos to go to a more rural—a less commercially and technologically advanced—country. "Eat your bread there. Prophesy there." Having already run down Amos as a second-rate fortuneteller, Amaziah now gives him back the title and function of prophet if only Amos will do it another place. In Cuba, perhaps, or Tasmania. The force of these words is not felt directly until Amaziah makes his edict: "never again prophesy at Bethel, for it is the king's sanctuary, and it is a temple of the kingdom."

What does that mean? As far as Amos is concerned, that is the only place to prophesy, because the controversy of God is not with the people but with Jeroboam, the king. Where else? As far as Amaziah is concerned it is the one place now off limits for Amos. Not only the place but the subject. A blunt translation of this edict is: You be quiet on the Assyrian issue. As of now, you are forbidden to touch the Assyrian issue.

And Amos. What does he say? Amos begins at the beginning. He answers Amaziah point by point. He admits, with a respectful amount of irony, as much as he thinks Amaziah can understand—as we are discovering in our President's present concern and virtual petulance over the fact that his popularity consensus in America is now below 50 per cent—with as much irony as he dares use, Amos says that indeed he is no prophet and he is not the son of a prophet. He does not fit into any niche. There is no way that the administration can get at him then. If he were a member of a prophets' guild, then he could be gotten at. But that is not the case. He is an independent man. His own man. His vocation is forestry and animal husbandry, a vocation that is far removed from the complications which an administration could throw in his way were his business, say, driving a taxi or selling merchandise of some kind. And also in these words, "I am a herdsman, and a dresser of sycamore trees," there is another dimension. Amos comes from the old Israel and is not a blooded born-and-raised city man so representative of the new slick Israel. Like his forefathers in the faith, he was a herdsman. Well, this is real irony because Amos, claiming his roots in the physical soil and the theological heritage of Israel, has made the sharpest points to be made about what went on in the city. He had seen what went on. He knew what went on. He knew the streets, far, far better than Amaziah. In one of his oracles Amos says:

Fire and Blackstone

Hear this, you who trample upon the needy, and bring the poor of the land to an end, saying, "When will the new moon be over, that we may sell grain? And the sabbath, that we may offer wheat for sale, that we may make the ephah small and the shekel great, and deal deceitfully with false balances, that we may buy the poor for silver and the needy for a pair of sandals, and sell the refuse of the wheat?" (Amos 8:4–6)

But this ironic introduction does not yet mean very much. He has so far only said that he is an independent man and nonorthodox. But that is not saying much. Amaziah, like any public figure, was no doubt constantly being informed of the activities of all of the nuts in town: the people who shout about the end of the world, and wear weird clothing, and make no impact at all on the populace. They are independent, too, and certainly nonorthodox. I came out of the subway on State Street just this week to be greeted by a bearded gentleman of approximately my age—an old man—dressed in the one pair of pants and shirt that he had been wearing constantly since he bought them secondhand in 1938, with a wire for a belt and no socks. A hype, really, pushing tracts for some change. The tract he handed me said, "You are going to hell." As I thought about the appointment I was rushing to, I speculated that he was entirely right but in a way he had not intended.

Anyway, Amos still had not said anything. So he took the great weight of Israel on his shoulders and said, "Yahweh God took me from following the flock, and Yahweh said to me: 'Go, prophesy to my people Israel.'" Without pride he said that. Quietly, simply, a matter of fact. Silence. Amos was saying that his credentials lay not in the *actuality* of his words, or in his public opposition to the administration, but in his calling. The words he said, as soon as they were spoken, would come into being not because they were true but because they were the words of Yahweh himself. In the presence of Amos, Amaziah was presented with the mouthpiece of the God of Israel.

Now Amos took up the one issue most dreaded by Amaziah: the Assyrian issue. Amos prophesied on the spot, and this does mean Amos was predicting like a two-bit fortuneteller: he was saying what had already been decided in the councils of heaven: "You [Amaziah] say, 'Do not prophesy against Israel, and do not preach against the house of Isaac.' Therefore thus says the Lord: 'Your wife shall be a harlot in the city, and your sons and your daughters shall fall by the sword, and your land shall be parceled out by line; you yourself shall die in an unclean land, and Israel shall surely go into exile away from its land.' "

Here was Israel in a period of unparalleled prosperity. Never had so few had so much. And over the horizon to the north Assyria was building one of the first really stupendous military juggernauts capable of capturing and ruling the world. The king and his counselors no doubt thought that they could accommodate themselves to Assyria. Work out mutually beneficial trade agreements to which would be attached integrity-of-national-boundaries clauses. Sure. The king was banking, no doubt, on his connections, his press releases, his friends. Namely on nothing. And Amos saw with unshatterable certainty that Assyria would roll over Israel while no one dared talk about the issue since it might upset the stock market and unsettle the populace.

Then Amos left the presence of Amaziah, his task accomplished. We hear nothing about Amos's feelings. We do not hear what the collector of his sayings did not see fit to tell us—whether or not Amos was fearful or angry or cool. That is not important. We do not hear how Amaziah reacted. That has no importance either. The importance lies in the confrontation itself. The practical king and Amos as the spokesman of Yahweh had a meeting in which the practical king said what he thought of Yahweh and the spokesman of Yahweh told the king what was going to happen.

We are long past that, you say. Very interesting historical lore back in the times before prophets started driving MGs and knew all about power structure and how to bend the Establishment toward courses favorable to the church. Very interesting, all right, but also blunt and direct in the force of its thrust into today's world. Our world. No Assyria on our horizon; only the specter of a mass revolt or what has been euphemistically called a riot against the intolerable everyday *circumstances* of daily life in a ghetto, *our* ghetto, this ghetto. As plain as the sun. The persistent harassment by arrogant merchants, the law-enforcement facilities, public-aid facilities and helping agencies and, yes, the grinding daily search for enough money, enough food, bail, a lawyer, a *way*, clothes. This will not go on because it cannot go on, and it cannot go on because once a certain limit of tolerance for pain and fear of reprisal has been passed there is open revolt. When nothing can be worse than now, *then* people rise up. And this is the clear picture today. This afternoon. Tonight, tomorrow, and Tuesday.

I think that all the forces of a twisted and viciously corrupt democracy are going to prevail on Tuesday. Despite the skilled impassioned work of devoted and talented believers in democracy in the Fifth Ward, despite the unnumerable hours, Tuesday midnight will see the machine in control.

We discovered an A.D.C. mother this week who had been visited by her precinct captain. He gave her a loyalty card to sign. This loyalty card stated clearly that if she did not vote a straight organization ticket her welfare checks would be stopped. This mother had doubts that the precinct captain could stop welfare checks. And she was disturbed. But not disturbed enough. Under no conditions would she reveal the contents of that loyalty card. We suggested that she appear on television behind a screen or with a pillow case over her head. Or mail the card to us or to Ab Mikva. She rejected every suggestion because she believes that the organization would find out. And she is just one of the numberless A.D.C. mothers who will be voting the straight ticket this Tuesday in fear. Absolute fear. Such fear will prevail on Tuesday and so will humiliation and so will riotous anger. For mark this well: after just so much of this treatment, mothers who presently are afraid of detection behind a screen will be out in the street burning up the place.

The pity is that the church occupies the position of Amaziah in this situation. It has cooperated nicely and is thus in no position to hear, much less to articulate this word. Therefore God has raised up, from no hill country but from the streets, his own prophetic voice. The Word of the Lord is today being spoken by the . . . poor. Amen.

5

BEWARE!

LUKE 12:13–21

The time has come. We debtors now overwhelmingly out-
number our creditors. We on the wrong side of bills, bill
collectors, notices that we are behind, please pay up; we
who have been so graciously allowed the use of borrowed
money and for the privilege pay insulting rates of interest;
we who have been driven half out of our minds with worry
sometimes over how we are ever going to get out alive: it is
time, I say, for us to take over. Up till now the seller has
gotten all the breaks. The rich man in Jesus's story had so
many breaks that he thought they would go on into eternity.
He thought he would be whisked away at death in a Silver
Cloud Rolls Royce to a private luxury hotel forever. That's
how it was and still is. The rich are the selling people. The
poor are the buying people. The selling people get all the
protection. The sellers can cheat you. Lie to you. Over-
charge you. Sell you merchandise that doesn't function and
you can't lay a glove on them. The law is in their favor.
Up till now, that is. Up till now, the quaint motto has been,
"Let the buyer beware." If the buyer is gulled, conned,
hustled, swindled, or just plain robbed—well, too bad for

him. He shouldn't be so dumb. A contract is a contract is a contract, the seller says, laughing all the way to the bank. Up till now. The time has come to change all that. We debtors have the power to put it the other way around, to reconstruct the economy so that it actually favors the buyer. All we need is a slight encouragement. Debtors surely have the wisdom. Now, what would a debtor-oriented economy look like?

The law would protect the buyer against the seller. Example: This week a man bought a 1962 automobile. It was slightly overpriced but in good shape. This particular make of automobile made few changes in 1962 over its 1961 model. A layman could not ordinarily tell what those changes were. Not the layman we are talking about. So in good faith he began signing papers for an ostensible 1962 car that, he discovered too late, was actually a 1961 car. He had been taken. The dealer smiled through his clenched teeth, a victory smile. In a debtor-oriented economy, the buyer would pick up the phone, call Third District police, have the seller of that car arrested and thrown into jail, fined, marched through the streets with a sign—"This man is a lying, cheating thief"—on his back, and then forced by law to revoke the contract or furnish the buyer with a 1962 automobile. As it is now, the buyer is merely paying $200, plus all that fabulous interest, more for an automobile than it is worth. Oh, tricky seller, beware. We are on to you and are learning how to deal with you. Someday we will have our laws, and until then what can we do? We can miss payments 1, 2, 3; pay 4 and promise 1, 2, 3, missing in the meanwhile, 5, 6, 7; renegotiate for lower payments; pay 1, miss 2, 3, 4 of the renegotiated contract; pay 5, and then, having actually paid two payments, pay no more until the automobile is repossessed. Let the bailiffs have it. Cheerfully. Serve Kool-Aid to the bailiffs who repossess and ask them what happened to the radio on that 1962 car, and the tires, and the wheels, and the carburetor, and the battery? Why that sign in vivid magenta paint on the back of the car, reading, "This is a 1961 Oldsmobile"? When the rest of us go to that dealer in real need of an automobile, do we take his word, his good-natured, bluff, hearty word, for anything? No. We are on our toes. We are good and suspicious. We bring along mechanic friends. We protect ourselves. Let the seller beware. We ask him for affidavits honorable in a court of law. We bring tape recorders so that we have a permanent record of the transaction on tape. Look. Under present circumstances very few people can purchase large merchandise, such as automobiles, with cash money. Most of us must buy on credit. We and the seller assume that the seller has the upper hand. He is granting us a favor to let us have an automobile. So he has the initiative, and he actually uses that initiative to intimidate. He practices the intimidation as he takes information necessary to discover our credit reliability. All of this is money to him because with such a precious psychological advantage he can overcharge and misrepresent, with you being made to feel that he is favoring you. But with tape recorders, mechanics, affidavits, and, yes, a Polaroid camera, and a lot of sharp friends, too, he is actually apt to be, if not himself intimidated, then wary. Let the seller beware. That is the thing we are after, wary enough to guard his words and make them somewhat true.

My friends, in my brief months among you I have been involved as third party and sometimes second party to a lot of credit installment negotiations. This is what I have found. The seller uses his credit check procedures as an intimidating device behind which screen he works the oldest flimflam in history. But I have also discovered that he is almost pitifully eager to sell. No matter what the credit check is, it seems, he will say O.K. He pays attention to one thing: your ability to pay. So, if you have a job at an establishment that seems rather secure, the merchandise is yours. The one thing the credit bureau cannot check on, or the seller, is your willingness to pay. You, at the point of paying, have the upper intimidating hand. You can be whimsically slow. Erratic. You can send in wrong amounts. Ask for renegotiations. In the important department of payment you are boss and not creditor, and do not forget it! The art of skating near the edge of repossession without actually falling in, unless it is to your advantage to do so, needs to be taught as a serious subject among debtors. Because until the law begins to read in favor of the debtor, thereby wiping out the legal advantage presently enjoyed by the seller, all we have to protect us is our wits . . . and our control of repayment.

On the point of laws. Senator Hart of Michigan has a bill hopelessly buried in committee that is called a truth-in-packaging bill. This bill would force merchandisers to state on the package in bold-size print how much actual stuff is inside. The buyer then could forget the size of the container, forget the stuff about King Size. The buyer could forget those strange formulae—5 Cents Off; Save 7 Cents—which do not mean anything since the merchandiser has not put down five cents off what or save seven cents off original purchase price of what. Forget all of that. Just look on the front of the package and see in prominent type how many ounces or pounds there are. Then see the plain price! That's fine. It makes packagers practice elementary honesty. Senator Douglas has a bill, also buried in committee, called a truth-in-lending bill. The provisions of this bill call for all credit installment institutions to tell you exactly how much the thing costs in itself and to tell you exactly how much they are taking for themselves outright, called carrying charges, for doing the paperwork, furnishing water coolers, free cups, free ashtrays, free chairs for you to sit in. Carrying charges, insurance charges, if any, and then *interest*. There you can see for yourself before ever you sign the contract that you are paying 24 per cent per annum or 22 per cent or 28 per cent. Not 6 per cent that *they* can borrow at or about 8 or 10 per cent if *you* went to the bank, but about three times that. Get the point? Senator Douglas believes that when people see that 24 per cent they will flip and just walk out. The credit people, faced with such shocking independence in their buyers, will have to begin charging decent rates or stop selling money.

There is another possible piece of legislation that we might conjure with. Its proposer is me. According to the provisions of this legislation, the actual amount of debt a citizen could incur would be set by law. A safe, reasonable amount determined by his income. Let us say 20 per cent. If he makes $5,000 a year, he can never have debt commitments over $1,000. Period. By law, then, every credit item would have to be reported. The information would go on a memory tape of an extra-huge electronic brain. When citizen X with the $5,000-a-year income makes a contact that puts him over his $1,000 limit, a big red light would begin flashing and twenty-four motorcycle policemen would roar out to the seller who made the contract and force him to tear up the contract or spend thirteen years in jail. I propose this legislation with generosity only in my heart: for the debtor. He would be protected against the creditor by law, and all moneymaking institutions would be furious because, despite their smiling talk about how people should not be overcommitted, they want the debtor to buy, buy, buy.

Yes they would be furious, just as they are furious with the truth-in-packaging and the truth-in-lending bills. Furious because this legislation might upset the outrageously large amounts and per-item profit they make. They are used to being protected. They are used to that motto, Let the buyer beware, and beneath their crafty hands, playing that shell game, there is only a heart full of pure greed. Think what they have going for them. They have the motto warning the buyer. So they can misrepresent, lie, cheat, *legally*. Then they next have the legal power to force the buyer to pay and, even more important, they have inserted inside the heads of all the buyers a little metaphysical judge who makes the life of the debtor miserable because he is in debt.

That is what I now want to deal with: that metaphysical judge who pronounces all debt wrong. He cannot stop you from incurring debt. But he can cause trouble until the debt is paid. This is all to the creditor's advantage. He has really got you in a vise between the repossessing bailiff on the one side and the stern judge on the other side.

Before the modern economy began to function at such a great clip, very few people were in serious debt. They owed small amounts here and there. Trade was vigorously on a cash or barter basis. In such an economy, debt was feared; also debtor's prisons, and society's vindictive judgments on people who got into debt and were not suitably prompt in repaying. It was constituted a mark against his character. Not in favor with man, he wasn't, it was subtly supposed, in very good favor with God. The creditors were in very, very good favor with God, of course. They who owed nothing. But the owers, debtors, borrowers, it was thought, had not shown sufficient enterprise, were not energetic enough, or were spiritually handicapped, not simply for being in debt but even more for not getting out of debt on the exact prescribed timetable. Of course, there is a religious dimension here. Of course, the Christian church has tried, to its everlasting shame, to identify God with that social judgment on debt, thus reinforcing the great power of the creditor-rich over the debtor-poor. But it doesn't hold up and never did. The judge inside the head is not a real judge. Not only is he not God, he is not a real judge. But he acts like one. He talks like one.

He can inspire guilt in us, we know that. He can create debt anxiety. Debt proneness. Debt worry. Debt depression. He can make us feel that our whole life is shaky and undermined. His accusing finger, held in a certain way, can cause strong and otherwise healthy adults to tremble and wilt and fall, and occasionally die; the note reading, among other things, "hopelessly in debt."

So who is this powerful figure in the middle of our head who acts and talks like a real judge? He has been sent by society to protect the interests of the creditor and has installed himself as a permanent part of the conscience, and as long as the debtor-poor never asked questions, never questioned the priority and superiority of the creditor-rich over the debtor-poor, this judgelike character could function smoothly and efficiently. Now we ask questions. The lines are no longer clear. We can see very prosperous fine people, not poor at all, out there in the marched-on areas. They live in a shadow poverty as real as the poverty we see in Oakland, or Woodlawn, or the West Side. This shadow poverty means an absence of live cash to buy with or to invest with. Why is there no cash when the family is making $25,000 a year? The family has this huge house with a mortgage, new furnishings, new car, new second car, new speedboat with twin Mercury engines, new color TVs, one for upstairs and down, new this and that. So that shoots the $25,000, and the daddy is hustling as hard as a Woodlawn daddy for tomorrow's grocery money. Heretofore this debt judgment, debt anxiety, was thought to exist in the exclusively Woodlawn areas. But now we look and lo, there is a shadow poverty in the land. There are fine people—white people, educated people, looked-up-to-people—who are hopelessly in debt, skating just on this side of repossession just like us, and this almost apocalyptic vision of black and white together sitting beneath the spurious judgment of a make-believe judge is enough to show that we have been hoaxed—bewitched, if you will; possessed, maybe—by a demon, masquerading as a godlike judge. Good friends, only if we assume money to be a part of a person, a literal part of him, can we assume that he is less good as a person because he is in debt; and we cannot do that. Money—owed, possessed, saved—money is still merely money: paper or metal, which, when procured or pledged, can secure goods and services. You cannot judge character by observing financial habits. You cannot knock a man's reputation as a man because of financial irregularity. A demon has taught us to do this. A demon, I suspect, sent by . . . business. It is this hocus-pocus, this demonlike possession, on which the most helpful word can be spoken. He has no legitimacy, this fraudulent judge. He will continue to speak angry words and wave his finger and try as best he can to make you feel depressed and guilty and anxious about being in debt. But he has no authority to speak and you have no business listening.

Let us put the matter this way: when creditors and debtors alike at the same time begin speaking true words to each other, then will be the time for creditors and debtors alike equally to honor true words and observe true commitments so that a pledge unfulfilled and a covenant violated are actions which breach the peace of the community. But until the seller stands with the buyer beneath this general banner of righteousness, a one-sided buyer practicing righteousness only encourages further rapaciousness in the seller. Let the church not only exorcise guilt-producing demons but in the great tradition of the prophets point out to all the people that God intends all men to speak and do truly as they deal with each other—that God has no favorites. The storekeeper is in no special zone of creation. He is a man. So, too, the moneylender, the banker, the auto salesman. They have no special prerogatives, no special exemptions from the demands of honesty.

In today's situation, with everything going for the creditor, so little for the debtor, it behooves the church to take the debtor's part until the scales are righted, justice is done, and economic brotherhood is a visible daily reality. Then the church may thank God for having brought about a good—not a great, a good—society and perhaps thereafter participate in that society as champion of neither creditor nor debtor but of man himself, as was the church's Lord. Amen.

6

DEAFNESS

ISAIAH 42:5–9   MATTHEW 9:27–34

This is a sermon to a people that has re-established its
composure. After all, our Mayor has expressed anger that
policemen did not shoot to kill arsonists, shoot to maim
adult looters, and Mace youth and child looters. A country
that can't seem to get the hang of listening. The text:
But just as Jesus and the Disciples were going out, some
people brought to him a dumb man who was possessed
by a demon. As soon as the demon was driven out, the
dumb man was able to speak. The crowds were amazed
and said, "Nothing like this was ever seen in Israel." The
morning and evening Jerusalem papers said, though, "It
is by aid of the Prince of Demons that he drives them out."

The crowd was impressed. Crowds are given to exag-
geration, we know. Wanting to be turned on. Corporate
responsibility is not the same as personal responsibility.
The crowd said specifically, "Nothing like this was ever
seen in Israel." That included the call to Abraham, Jacob
wearing bearskin hands to fool father Isaac, burning bushes,
crossing the Red Sea, David, Elijah making the fire burn
though drenched with water—three times—I mean, Israel

had seen a lot, yet the crowd on that occasion said, "Nothing like this was ever seen in Israel." Very impressed. Now Jesus had healed a number of people. He had raised a little girl from apparent death. He had just healed a blind man, remember. The crowd was talking about *all* of these events. But especially about the last. The crowd dug that mute man talking. Note next the reaction of public opinion. The Pharisees. The newspapers. The Fuzz. Who did not like the idea at all. Jesus was mysterious and in a vague way threatening. They have an election coming up, maybe, or are beginning to worry about the summer. Stokely may be in town any day. At any rate, the dead should stay dead. The blind should stay blind. The mute should stay mute. I mean, things should stay glued together and nailed down. The Fuzz doesn't believe in messing around with the way things are. Innovation should always be spelled T-R-O-U-B-L-E. So they develop a theory to explain the events which so impressed the crowds; the boys in the back room start to fiddle with scare words in headline combinations. You know: "Prince of Demons Jesus's Pal" "Satan and Jesus Paint Town Red" and so on. The official line was meant to discredit Jesus and thereby to get the crowd safely back in line.

The text makes clear the reaction of the crowd first and the Pharisees second in order to emphasize how dramatic these healings were. Especially the last. Especially the healing of the mute man. I presume because his plight was so much less vivid. The apparently dead girl. The blind man. These are so impossible. But a mute man can, after all, function. He can use all his limbs. He can see and hear. He can take orders and work. By using his hands he can communicate, fairly well, on a basic level. He is not in too bad shape. All that is wrong with him is that he cannot talk. Considering what most people do with their ability to talk, that is not a great disability. He is maybe better off, and so on. But because it is not your championship-type trouble like death or blindness, and because of what muteness is in itself, popular reaction was instant and enthusiastic when Jesus healed the mute man. Because of what muteness is in itself.

I got stepped on by a cleated football shoe many decades ago and had to be stitched up, which required tape all over my face to immobilize my mouth where the stitches were. For six days I was mute. At first it was a novelty. Almost fun. All listening and no talking. Very soon the novelty wore off. People began speaking for me, I noticed. I could listen to discussion but could not join. Because I could not talk even in that short period, my friends and family, it seemed, almost acted as though I could not hear either. At the beginning I found myself framing responses, in conversations going on around me, which could not be used. But soon I was not thinking any responses. My inability to talk had cut some deep nerve. I was only a watcher of the action. I wasn't in on the action. It was a moving experience, being mute. For weeks after the tape was removed I still was not functioning at previous high-talking levels. It took that long to reassume an active position in the life around me. Muteness in itself is a terrible handicap precisely because it isn't terrible, because people do not think it is terrible. To be inarticulate in a very talky human life means something specific. You don't have any say. You cannot protest. You cannot affirm. You cannot question. You cannot answer questions. What remains? The crude business of simple yeses and noes. Left or right. This or that. Human beings in speaking with one another negotiate meaning. Very few pure yeses or pure noes. Lefts or rights. But something in between that cannot be easily explained. More than that, the things most worth saying do not come at the beginning but toward the end of conversation, after the stock stuff has been trotted out, and after a pattern of meaning has been established. All of which is denied a mute person. He cannot respond; therefore people tend to talk at him. They begin not to think of him as a complicated person like they are, but as something simpler. If you want the truth of it, they begin to treat him like an idiot. Because of what muteness is in itself, when Jesus drove the demon inhibiting a mute man's speech out, and the mute man could talk freely, there was instant and enthusiastic response. From the crowd. And a flurry of activity at City Hall. As we have seen.

All right. As L.B.J. and Ho said this week, "Let's escalate" this not talking. Only a crude and merciless fundamentalism would limit this text to the physically handicapped, to those people born without vocal chords or with deformed sound-forming abilities. The text rules in all mutes. Those who sit in stunned perpetual silence. Those who have been beaten down into virtual silence. Those who have nothing to say because they have never been listened to. Those who are unable to talk. The functioning mute as well as the congenital mute. The spiritual mute for whom human speech is yes, no, left, right. They do not protest or affirm. They neither question nor are questioned. The voiceless. Have you any idea what a vast number of the human race we are naming? The whole third world, with certain notable exceptions. The great majority of human beings on this earth, only a few decades ago savages, natives, by the millions, utterly without voice. Considered by the Christian West as incapable of civilized speech and by the millions, whole constellations of colored peoples residing in sequestered living spaces—ghettoes. Because of where they are and what color they are, their voice has been ignored, muted, totally unheard. Functioning mutes. I am speaking here of political voicelessness. And I am suggesting that you followers of Jesus have mercy on the mute.

I lay it as a matter of exceptional concern on you inasmuch as we have such a text before us.

We do mean more than political voicelessness, but we also mean political voicelessness. So let us deal with that kind of muteness first. It is clear in the ongoing fuss over rioting, e.g., who has voice and who is pretty voiceless. When the fuming Mayor of Chicago spoke this week about shooting to kill . . . et cetera . . . he was heard all right, on page one, on all TV channels, and especially in the hearts of his white countrymen. His police listened; his judges listened; his jailers listened; his school board listened; the nation listened (aghast for the most part, but listened). There were other voices heard vigorously opposing the order in behalf of those who were targets of the Mayor's wrath. Leaders spoke out. Big names grabbed headlines. And the people? Well, they didn't quite make it. I don't know how many reporters called me up, visited, wanting me to sum up, represent, project for: as though the people, the vast nameless people, who all look alike, had nothing to say or maybe cannot talk. So Chicago moves on toward catastrophe. As do, I suppose, Nashville, and Newark, and about the whole of metropolitan U.S.

These people *can* talk. Now there is political voicelessness, and there is another example, too. You have been reading in the papers about Teen Murder, Inc. You have been hearing and reading since September about these older fellows who hire younger fellows to kill. You have heard the names Paul Martin, Eugene Hairston, Jeff Fort. You have heard the spectacular array of charges against them, treated always with insulting certainty of their guilt. Without any new reason, some papers just keep reviewing the routine. Who has the voice? The G.I.U., the Assistant State's Attorney. The same group who were vigorous opponents of busing, who defended the Mayor's hard line, opposed these young men. Yes, they have hard and raucous voices, and they were heard. From the three accused: not one word. Mute. No matter how forcibly they affirmed their innocence and protested the charges against themselves, no judge listened, no citizens listened. Mute. Well, the first of these youths was finally tried on seven counts of murder. And after a five-day trial the jury deliberated for about one hour and returned to find Paul Martin not guilty on all charges. Did anyone read that in the paper? Did anyone hear the mighty cry of joy from the vindicated? Did reporters interview a man held without bail for 125 days and deprived of his ordinary human community? No. What can *he* have to say? A functioning mute. Had the jury found him guilty, of course, the great voices would have been heard. Yes. The news of his guilt would have crowded presidential politics off the headlines. And when youth number two was later tried, the same slapstick routine was followed. The same dreary round of voiced allegations, the same not guilty, and the same voicelessness. This is political voicelessness, and I lay it as a concern before you: because of what happens to a person who cannot make himself heard; because he inevitably turns in rage away from humankind or subtly becomes less of a man than is indicated merely by his voicelessness. Less and less able to affirm, protest, question, share, intimate, laugh, encourage, reminisce, and make vows. I lay it as a concern before you because it was a concern of Jesus, and you are his followers to do his work in this present world.

But we are here dealing with more than political voicelessness. We are dealing with the muteness far beyond all political social constructions as a very threat to human existence itself. Well do the scriptures term this the work of demons, the enemies of life, the messengers of death. Muteness is a prefiguring of death from where no sound emerges. The autistic child and the adult in a catatonic trance are merely more advanced models of the muteness that seizes the beings of people throughout the civilization. People who cannot talk, who cannot and do not express themselves. Who have no witty repartee, no snappy comeback. Who dare not betray their inarticulateness. Some of whom are too angry to talk. Some of whom, alas, have nothing to say because their souls have shriveled. It is to these people I call your attention. It is concern for them, mandated by the mighty Lord Jesus, that I lay upon you. This is the fundamental task before you as a Christian congregation, a summation of the Christian mission. Because in exorcising these demons you rid human beings of the chill hand of death, you raise them from an imputed idiocy into full human stature. You give them back their voice, and this requires special power, on the order of Eastern religious figures who can jump into a driving river in the middle of winter and make their temperature rise. On the order of Elijah, who could make the drenched wood catch on fire. On the order of shamen, wizards, the bizarre and eccentrically powerful. On the order but not them. No. Their power but not their style. The style has been mandated and cannot be improvised. And what is this mandated style so christologically fixed? To make total identification with the voiceless, not in order to lend them voice, which is the offensive and abusive tactic of white liberalism in the church these days, not in order to lend them voice, but for the purpose of exorcism: to the one predominating end that the mute talk.

Can you envision that? Can you envision the ghetto talking? Have you any idea of the wealth of rich and intricate and utterly humanizing sounds are there to be uttered? Have you any notion of the denseness and intensity of rage? What do verbal Molotov cocktails sound like? What would the ears do with these stunningly articulated dreams, these verbal creations of sorrow and sequestration? The end of exorcism is sound: *creative sound*. Human speech from the no longer voiceless.

I had thought that the national agony following the death of Martin Luther King might have mobilized the church to make the fateful move across the DMZ to stand inalterably, once for all, with the colored poor and there be joyfully enveloped with creative explication, with exuberant hopeful speech. But no such thing happened, of course. The arrogant and merciless church can hear nothing but its own ponderous litanies of guilt in hastily conceived memorial services carried off in maximum bad faith.

The mandated style is identical for private Christians, for Christian congregations, for Christian institutions. Without qualification. Without exception. The Christian church faces, after all, in this terrible crisis the possibility of identifying with the colored poor or of being pastor and special adviser to an unchastened white power with genocide on its mind. The one possibility lies in the zone of faithfulness. The other lies in the zone of apostasy.

So, good Christian people, rejoice today in the happy recall of the man who was delivered from his muteness and restored to his true humanity. Yes, rejoice and be assured that the mute are and will increasingly be found speaking, whether with or against a befuddled, guilty, and very white church. Amen.

7

SUPERTRUMPING

DEUTERONOMY 29:16–29   MARK 13:9–27

In order to clarify the deep intent of the two Biblical passages you have just heard, I want to introduce you to the following situation. You are playing bridge. You are North. East is playing a five-spade contract. He is playing from his hand. He has the ace of spades and two good diamonds in the dummy, which locks up his contract. With the same kind of confidence that Vince Lombardi has about this afternoon, East leads out a little spade. South throws on his last trump. Up comes the big ace from the dummy. This arrogant East hardly waits to see what you will play. It is a good thing. Because you then play the ace of—well, not spades or hearts or diamonds or clubs. What is that the ace of? It is a Purple Dragon. It is the ace of supertrumps. It trumps any named trumps. So you take the trick; your two hearts are good. North is down three. Except not really. North, South, East, and West are down farther than that. You are all down so far that you are out of the game of bridge. By that brilliant maneuver of introducing your Ace of the Purple Dragon as supertrumps, you also introduced something beyond bridge, something which overrules and destroys bridge.

Something which is a new game played strictly within fantasy life, a bigger game, a majestic game in which stated powers are put down.

There was once a famous conference for campus pastors across the country who, among other things, had daily study sessions on the book of Amos, led by competent Old Testament specialists. To my knowledge the best game of supertrumps was played there. One of these pastors in one of these study sections made casual mention of the theory of Henry Norris Paine, a prominent Amos specialist. The discussion leader, an Old Testament specialist in his own right, was just insecure enough to be puzzled, and in order to cover himself he pretended in a noncommittal sort of way that there was such a specialist who had that theory, although this section leader had never heard of him, and nobody in the world had either because the campus pastor, our hero, had just that moment made the name up. After the section meeting he began holding forth at the dinner table and in late-night bull sessions on the theories of Professor Henry Norris Paine. So other sections began to consider these theories, and other section leaders were drawn in, too insecure to admit that *they*, authorities *paid* by the conference to be experts, had never heard of such an eminent name. So the whole conference came to accept without challenge the theory that the book of Amos was written in the second century B.C. by a Hellenistic Jew, the theory developed by the great New Zealand Old Testament scholar named Henry Norris Paine. Our hero, during the last meal of the conference, read a summary of the national and international news—a custom made necessary because the conference was being held in the deep sticks some place—and one of his items was that Dr. Henry Norris Paine, world-renowned New Zealand authority on the book of Amos, had passed away just the day before. Our hero suggested they all stand

for a moment of silence and only then did it begin to
dawn on the conference, one at a time but in growing
waves of incredulous laughter, that they had been gulled.
That the Ace of the Purple Dragon had been played. That
they had been supertrumped. That this name-dropping,
prestige-seeking, authority-quoting bunch had been taken.
Put down by our hero of zero cool. In just such a way
that ever after none of those conferees dared admit that
they knew something or had read a book or had heard
of a theory unless they really knew it or had read it or
had heard of it. The name of the game is supertrumps.
It is played daily by people reaching for a little more
clout to add to their own views, threats, predictions,
or theories.

Now in the Old Testament lection we have the threat
of a curse coming down on any individual or the whole
people of God who have made any kind of commitment
to one of these foreign gods . . . these—idols. So much
as a secret commitment will bring on the curse. One
need not openly declare appreciation for one of these
foreign gods, or curiosity, or, much less, allegiance. It
can be perfectly secret, all the while that the individual
or the people maintain scrupulous faithfulness to the
sworn Covenant with Yahweh, the God of Israel. But
that doesn't matter to Yahweh, says this writer. The secret
is known by Yahweh, and his anger is not therefore moderated. He will curse the individual, the individuals, or the
entire people. Later generations will look upon the "whole
land brimstone and salt, a burnt-out waste, unsown, and
growing nothing, where no grass can sprout [just like
Sodom and Gomorrah]" and see the wreckage, and they
will shake their heads and know that the ruin was the
work of Yahweh against a people who forsook the Covenant. This kind of Old Testament writing is known as
character-building. It is similar to the dire imprecations

parents hurl at children that if they do not blah, blah, blah, then the parents will beat them within an inch of their lives or keep them in or punish them in other fantastic ways. The aim is to produce in the hearer such fear of unutterable consequences that he will refrain from ever doing this specified activity. And the writers of this passage have enlisted truly cosmic powers, not merely the Ace of the Purple Dragon but Purple Dragons themselves, as potential agents of destruction. The writers want us readers to shudder at these dread consequences. And in that shuddering they want us to avoid this proscribed activity, which is showing secret interest or allegiance to any other gods.

And in the New Testament lection, eternal hope is held out to the small band of persecuted Christians that *they* will be saved and no others when the approaching cataclysm takes place. Then "the sun will be darkened, and the moon will not give its light, and the stars will be falling from heaven, and the powers in the heavens will be shaken." Then will appear "the Son of man coming in clouds with great power and glory. And then he will send out the angels, and gather his elect from the four winds, from the ends of the earth to the ends of heaven." Christ is a hope to place in your heart. An eternal solace. You live under this totalitarianism or that and suffer. And will continue to suffer the inhumanities practiced on you. Look toward any structure in the world and you will find only an old or a new or a potential totalitarianism, eager to enslave you, to rob and beat you, to practice its greed on you. But look beyond, into the great and unnamable future, to a time known only to God, and there affix your hope, for in that time the godly powers which created all worldly powers will smash them and elevate all the lowly and misused, all the Christians who have endured faithful to the end.

Certainly this writing was intended to produce hope in an utterly hopeless situation. It said to persecuted Christians that they must hold fast. It said to suffering Christians that they must look beyond any present suffering to their eternal health. An eternal hope thus generated the strength required of Christianity to endure totalitarianisms until it could itself become one and dominate the Western world—as it did for fully a millennium.

These two Bible writings were successful in what they intended to do—but were objectively untrue. The Son of man did not come on clouds of glory to save those battered and trembling Christians. They just got gobbled up by the lions, by Nero's fire, and by . . . eventual success. Likewise many Hebrews who had harbored secret admiration for foreign gods died contented old men whose fields were certainly not destroyed. Which leads us to see that the Biblical writers are not above the use of highest authorities in making threats *or* promises. And in many sections of Christendom present-day Christian leaders employ the weight of Christ's name to ensure the success of their projects: moral projects or building projects, the Fifty Million Fund. And in many other sections of Christendom the mighty authority of Christ, the author of "The Right" or "The Truth," is used to promise utter revolution or to hold it back. I am not suggesting that this is a cynical use of the divine name, or a calculated use. These people—as surely as the Biblical writers—believe fully in what they are predicting. They first screw their credulousness up to its breaking point, then in great passion make these big threats or big promises. Not a cynical use of the divine name, but a misuse, nonetheless. Perhaps this is not the encouragement we need right now, but it is encouraging, all the same, to find that Christians differ little from other people and are not above supertrumping whenever it comes in handy. An eternal Ace. We are God's people.

Fire and Blackstone

What we do is right because it is a right we have learned from God. That is just plain supertrumping. Why? Because we dare not say the truth, the literal, actual truth, which is: What we do is what we *understand* to be right and can be wrong.

I have been impressed once more this week by the intricate authority system employed by the official city of Chicago in attempting to embarrass or harass the First Presbyterian Church. I thus call your attention to last Tuesday afternoon. Owing to a series of wild rumors, some of the young men in the neighborhood began shooting at each other. The police arrived and came into the church, insisting that an unidentified adult female citizen had seen a group of young men running into the church with guns. They were supertrumping. They had no search warrant, so they had to produce the authority they needed, which was the hot-pursuit provision of the search law. They alleged they were in hot pursuit and therefore could enter. Once in they showed no haste. This was perhaps cool hot pursuit. They were interested in discovering something that might be used to embarrass us. And they did find an old, unusable .22 rifle, rusty, begrimed, in such a place and under so much grime that I believe it was left behind by those W.P.A. writers who I learned Wednesday night used the church during the late thirties. Also a curious piece of pipe was found, which instantly was named by the glorious name "bomb." This is supertrumping, also. No expert opinion might be introduced. If they say it is a bomb, it is. A box of .22-caliber ammunition was also discovered exactly in the place where it had been put after being found one day. So this cache of weapons, discovered after a minute search of the building, was then taken outside where the summoned press was waiting. More supertrumping. The press was presented with an elaborate theory made up to fit what they had in their hands, and the press responded like the good little papers they are. Who are they to question the mighty experts of the mighty law enforcement wing of the mighty Democratic machine in Chicago? So, good friends, we are supertrumped. An authority higher than the authority of common sense or the authority of law—namely, the authority of flat-out racism—was used. The Ace of the Purple Dragon fell. They took the trick and wrenched once more the weak and febrile hopes any of us have that there can ever be law and order in this or any other ghetto.

What is the temptation? For us to use an even higher authority than the highest authority in Chicago; to be blunt, to use the name of God in retaliation. To threaten. Bluster. Shout. Phone up the press and be very angry. You know, blow our top, but in such a way that our right is defended and also in such a way that God's right is identified with our right. Then the supertrumps are trumped by super supertrumps. No. That may be a temptation, good people, but it does not match the facts, or the truth about the situation.

Supertrumping as an activity is also destructive of human beings, even when used in the Bible, and certainly when it is used as a means to beat people down. It is the technique of a bully. It is indigenous to fascism and is in fact the very methodology most descriptive of fascism. Our eyes as well as our historical senses tell us with unchangeable certainty that this technique wrecks human beings and human communities. It denies the possibility of error and fallibility in authorities, be they state or church. After all, what we know for sure we know for sure and can tell why. And what we know but with less certainty cannot be made more certain by the use of a night stick or gun or a Holy Bible. And what we are puzzled about does not clear itself up just because we ignore part of the puzzle in order to achieve clarity and certainty. Furthermore, there must be maintained among us human beings a distinction between what we know for sure, what we know but not for sure, and what we are puzzled about. Bluffing or supertrumping does not actually change those distinctions. It changes any who use such techniques into bullies and brutes, however. And adds to the constant totalitarian pressures that mankind is ever under.

I think there is a role for the church . . . this church . . . in this bizarre age and even more bizarre city here and now. This role is to call into question every authority—law enforcement, courts, the political apparatus, the Mayor, realtors, the welfare Establishment, the Board of Education, local school officials—in such a way that they are made to produce the bases for their decisions and policies, and if it appears that they justify their decisions on the basis of their power alone—the essence of supertrumping—then let this fact be known. Notice the role I suggest does not involve, immediately at least, the proposal of alternative policies. Our role is not to shout God while they shout that they are the regularly appointed experts. Our role is somehow to slow down the shouting so that it can become clear to all what is for sure, what is pretty sure, and what is puzzling. And an important part of this role is to produce, to have actual programs, so that we need not shout or propose but have only to point. These actual programs then become authoritative because they work.

And the hope involved in this role is a hope based solidly in the life and ministry of our Lord Jesus and the humanity he taught us to serve. Our hope then is not that dirty fascist dogs will be wiped out by thunder-bolts or by rhetoric or any loud shouting on our part. That is a comforting thing to know. They will be put down by people who are determined only by what serves people and who thus upset their oppressors. Our hope is in people and in saving people and in living with people. Our hope is in human trust established humbly in performance, which is another way of saying our hope is in the Lord Jesus.

I want to be quite clear, because we are faced with enormously powerful and practiced supertrumpers. Let us, then, be prepared to say out loud and quite calmly that the Ace of the Purple Dragon can't take tricks because there is no such thing. Say to policemen who exceed the law that they are lawbreakers. To state's attorneys who use the press to win cases that the proper place for trials is before juries. To juries that the only basis for a verdict is evidence, documented believable evidence. And to the schools that education of children, and not busing or nonbusing or how much, is the issue. And to all: that authority cannot be granted but must be demonstrated. And in entering these matters we shall well serve not only ourselves and our blessed reputation but simply thousands of people whose spirits had fallen victim to the Purple Dragon but have risen and are shining because they see that Purple Dragons cannot be played. Amen.

PART THREE

Black Power and Christian Responsibility

8

BLACK POWER AND CHRISTIAN RESPONSIBILITY

The backlash is on. A good many white people have reasserted their superiority. They are going to stop these . . . ah . . . niggers marching around. They are going to stop this drift, this Negro coddling, all of this attention to Martin Luther King, these giveaway programs of Federal tax money to Negro mothers who go on having babies so they can get bigger welfare checks. They are going to stop these laws, too, these housing laws. And more than all else, they are going to see to it that law and order return to our once proud and sane land. Therefore we have quite a new cast of characters on the political scene who have subtly told these backlash voters that they don't like colored folks, either. It has been happening since Watts, really, when the raw cadences of "Burn, Baby, Burn" got a national hearing, building up through this last

---

I delivered this address in Milwaukee to a joint meeting of an inner city and a suburban congregation on November 10, 1966, the very evening when the Chicago police were conducting their first major raid on the First Presbyterian Church of Chicago.

summer, but surfacing hard Tuesday. White folks have said "enough!" to the mild American flirtation with the civil rights movement. In Cleveland, you know, there is an organization called the N.A.A.W.P., poor things, whose cause so desperately needs advancing.

Now let's try to get some perspective on this backlash. It is not a condemnable item that will go away with a few choice paragraphs of Supreme Court rhetoric. It is a signal to black people in America: "Your nonviolent marchers have angered us. Your riots have nauseated us. You thought you could force your way into our suburban life. Well, you are wrong. You can't. So lay off; go on back to your ghettoes and be quiet." It is important that we see this message being signaled to black people. It is also important to see that this is the *only* message from the white to the black community. Many white people do not want to be associated with this fresh appearance of white power. Well, with few exceptions, there has been a great silence from this sector. So what else is the black community to believe?

Let me illustrate. The Presbytery of Chicago last Tuesday night had a serious controversy over a document called *A Manifesto in the Face of a Backlash*. This document had been prepared by the Chicago Presbyterian Interracial Council chapter. Its attempt was to reaffirm the historic position of the Presbytery *then*, while the vote was being counted, and to have every pastor read this manifesto from his pulpit next Sunday. Let me read some sections so that you can get its flavor.

Our denomination, our Synod, our Presbytery, and particular churches, before the backlash, believed with evident conviction —citing Biblical-theological grounds in abundance—that racial segregation in *any* form was sinful. Now that the backlash is upon us, has racial segregation in its many forms become less sinful? Before the backlash we asserted the primacy of the living human being, no matter of what race; we asserted his essential dignity, his necessary standing place within the community of man. Have these assertions now become so problematic that the Church can no longer truthfully attest to their validity? We have repeatedly expressed repugnance at closed neighborhoods and have as repeatedly called on this community to adopt an all-out policy of non-discriminatory, open-occupancy housing. Are closed neighborhoods now more attractive and open housing less worthy of support simply because bigots have begun shouting at us? We have heretofore been the champions of the poor and espoused their legitimate desires to secure adequate living environments. Are they suddenly so well off, their housing so miraculously improved, their neighborhoods so well cared for that they no longer need our support? We have in past times decried the evils of de facto segregation. Has de facto segregation something new to commend it and have the evils of thousands of Negro children in Chicago and suburbs diminished because it is now not safe to point out these evils? We have announced ourselves the friend of the Negro in countless ways. But in the face of the backlash we are tempted to pass him by quickly on the other side of the street, fearing that our white friends will notice the friendship.

It is our desire, as the Presbytery of Chicago, to reaffirm on this date our determination to continue to support the struggle for justice and equal opportunity. We hereby reaffirm our desire for an Open City and an Open Metropolis. We cannot wait until it is once more safe to be counted on the side of the Negro community. We cannot wait out the white fury and then convince the poor, the Negro, the minority citizen, that we have been their friends all along.

Let us now, before God and our neighbors, reaffirm our witness for justice and equal rights in this place and time. Let us, solemnly and fully, take our place in the midst of the Negro and other minority citizens of Chicago, suffering with them, striving with them for a permanent respite from the oppression they undergo at the hands of a sinful community. We must take sides until . . . there are no more sides. Let our side be against the backlash, unequivocally, joyfully, solemnly, from this day forth.*

* *From* A Manifesto in the Face of a Backlash, *presented November 8, 1966.*

Fire and Blackstone

Now everyone who spoke against the manifesto tried to mark himself off clearly from bigotry and backlash. These pastors did not want their people to hear what Presbytery's position had been all along. Especially on pledge Sunday, as they all got around to saying. It was clear that they considered the United Presbyterian Church to be a white institution, and it was clear that they felt themselves called on to protest the sensibilities of their white constituents. Now I am not interested here in the moral flabbiness of this fact. I am illustrating the character of the liberal silence in the face of the backlash. I am saying that what the black man hears, and sees, feels, and believes right now is white power. The iron fist without the velvet glove.

The mere polite long-distance signaling is significantly inflammatory to the black community. But let us add a further dimension; namely, the very tough police policy now operative in Negro ghettoes throughout metropolitan U.S. "Law and order" is the way the slogan goes. Furious citizens have demanded of their police departments any kind of procedures necessary to stop those riots and make America safe for democracy, safe for little old ladies again. In the curious thinking of these infuriated citizens, the people in Watts or West Side Chicago were getting arrogant. They had been seeing too much television with M.L.K. and L.B.J. Too many colored people on TV and in the papers. So they got out of line. Tried to take the law in their own hands. What are we going to do? Club 'em back into the ghetto and keep 'em there. There is nothing new about police abuse of Negro citizens. It has been a steady ingredient of Negro life in America since go. It used to be just ordinary sadism. Now it is something more. William Stringfellow calls attention to this something more. He calls it a new police militarism. Police are acting more and more like occupation forces dealing with an alien people. Negro citizens are thus treated daily to indignities and violations of constitutional rights by policemen who—in the dark and outside the eye of CBS TV—make Bull Connors seem law-abiding. They have been given this license by the white community, which has effectively communicated its fear and distress to its own political leaders, who have communicated get-tough orders to police superintendents and so on. So for the black man on the street the backlash is more than a political word for the *New York Times* to fuss with. To him the backlash is a very mean and tough police force. I could tell you some pretty rough stories, but then you might think it a play on your sympathies or consider it sensationalist grandstanding. Tonight we shall only deal with abstract gore, not doubting for a moment, however, the existence of gore.

Well. Just ordinary Negro people have never believed too much in all the civil rights stuff, anyway. They know too much the way it really is, are too skeptical of laws, accords, agreements, in the face of continuing persecution and denial. But for a few years the heat was a little bit off, and they were grateful for that. Just ordinary Negroes—not especially gifted, not morally sensitive—they felt that the Stokely Carmichael–Floyd McKissick type of black power was more civil rights sloganeering. They haven't wanted necessarily to get Whitey—not because they didn't dislike him, because they did and do dislike him, but because Whitey had more guns and it was no use to try to get him. Ordinary Negroes have mistrusted the ballot box about as much as they have the police, as another white game. So the S.N.C.C. sort of black power, which so alarmed America, hasn't really any chance of becoming operational in the Negro soul. But the backlash has producd something quite different that I think we must consider here tonight.

Fire and Blackstone

Black power in the ghetto is mostly diffuse. There are a lot of angry people capable of bloc voting, capable of staging a protracted, skillful, guerrilla-type riot. It is, as I say, diffuse. They do not respect the neofascist type of law and order that should be inhibiting their riotous instinct. That is not the point. The anger has not been collected, focused, structured. It is surely there, just waiting. As such it is potential black power that becomes actual when it is massed and then provoked. But not all anger is diffuse. Some has been collected and organized, and the name of this is teen-aged gangs. Generally these gangs are very tough, destructive, very violent. They have guns and knives. They mostly fight among themselves. But suddenly in this backlashed situation they are beginning to consider what their fathers and mothers may never have openly considered: namely, a full-swing revolt. A war, not a riot. Not an incident that thirty patrol cars can put down, but a war.

Let me illustrate again. There are on Chicago's South and West Sides four major constellations of gangs: the Vicelords, Cobras, Devil's Disciples, and Blackstone Rangers. They have shifting alliances and historic animosities. But recently the big leaders of these four gang constellations have been meeting privately in order to talk things over. And what do you think they talk about? A basketball league? No. You are wrong. What is the matter with the Bears? Wrong again. They are talking about how they can create a series of incidents in such a way that the Mayor would be forced to call in the National Guard, and then they would openly invite the colored boys in the Guard to join them! What a nonsense plan. Right, it is nonsense because it is unimaginable. But, you know, from my intimate knowledge of one of these gangs, and hence my knowledge of their organizational skill, I have got to say that it might work. This is merely illustrative of black power, please, and not a prediction meant to frighten anyone.

Well, these are fabulously cool young men. I was lately reading Norman O. Brown's book, *Love's Body*,* and was startled by the following passage:

> The energy which builds fraternal organization is in rebellion against the family and the father; it is youthful energy. Ortega y Gasset can see that the primeval political association is the secret society, not the gray-bearded senate, because he is willing to acknowledge the youthful, or sportive, or playful origin of the state. "It was not," he says, "the worker, the intellectual, the priest, properly speaking, or the business man who started the great political process, but youth, preoccupied with women and resolved to fight—the lover, the warrior, the athlete." The ideology of utilitarianism, which is the origin of the state and everywhere in life sees only obedience to necessity and the satisfaction of elementary vital needs, is senile, and in politics sees only senatorial activity. Youthful energy has that exuberance which overflows the confines of elementary necessity, and rises above labor into the higher, or is it lower, sphere of play. (Ortega y Gasset, "The Sportive Origin of the State," 32)
>
> Academic orthodoxy, senile and senatorial, is against fraternities; against Sparta; against Plato; against athletics; against play; against sex; against youth. "The fate of the sons," says Freud, "was a hard one; if they excited the father's jealousy they were killed or castrated or driven out."

Startled because I thought instantly of the Blackstone Rangers. They are really interested in remaking Woodlawn. They do no longer trust the despotic old arteriosclerotic adult world. They are not as yet castrated. They believe in nothing but themselves: their own strength, their own intelligence, their own beauty, their own future. They came to peak strength during the backlash and thus represent to me the real black power in America today. Scary. Risky and hopeful.

* *New York: Random House, 1966.*

It would be very nice if only there weren't so much violence in the picture. But there is plenty of violence in the backlash and even more violence in the black-power responses to this last-straw white-power display.

As a theologian, pastor, and plain American, I wish the church could exercise its Christian responsibility in two ways: First, that it could somehow moderate the force of the backlash, and, second, inform black power of policy options involving low degrees of violence. I wish it, and I recommend both exercises of Christian responsibility. But I don't for a minute believe that Christians will do either, meaning by Christians people who go to churches. People who go to churches are frightened out of their heads mostly, if they know anything, and mostly indifferent because they know *nothing*. They are on the side of the backlash and can hardly, from that compromised position, hope to moderate it. And on the other side the Christians who go to churches located in black-power areas—ghettoes—have such a history of colonialism that they have a difficult time making themselves credible to these cool young men.

So what does a Christian responsibility do, then, with the best intentions in the world if it cannot perform? There is one thing it can do and I believe, bluntly, must do, and that is to give itself up. It is too old anyway. It needs to be retired. Do you know what? I am sick of Christian responsibility. I have found secular responsibility much more responsible and Christian irresponsibility much too inviting. I do not believe in Christian responsibility. I suggest something quite different, something bizarre, something that Christian responsibility would label insane: namely, a joyous, very mellow, go-for-broke split from the whole responsibility scene. Responsibility is one way to say white power, and it is this cultural rape of the Christian Gospel that I am calling your attention to by suggesting wilder, riskier, more heavenly nonresponsibility.

Nonresponsibility, not caring for the morrow, e.g., not really caring about all of those things that inhibit cunning and violent action. You see pastors who do not think about all of those bad words and angry scowls but stand right up and say it out loud. Say that the issues of one hundred years of terrible, unspeakable injustice to the Negro people have come now into open clarity. I take my place beside my Negro brothers and invite you to join me. Now this is plain nonresponsibility. Insane. Especially on budget-making day. And back in the ghetto, nonresponsibility means digging right in on those great young men, staying with them, facing the terror they daily face, feeling the pressure—the hunger—they daily feel, feeling with them along a dark wall on a dark night as they make their run for the daylight; i.e., pushing them hard to make the full range of their dreams come true, no matter what the Mayor or the Presbytery or the police force thinks. It is strictly nonresponsibility, appalling, too hard even to consider, but it is the way, the one credible way, open to Christians today.

I wish I had a nice upbeat coda to play now, some way to say "I'm only fooling, we still live in a great community and have a great church and those Negroes aren't really mad." But no such lying words are available. I have not come to Milwaukee in the middle of a serious crisis to tell lies. I have tried to tell the way it is. God be merciful to us all.

9

GILLS

Jeremiah 20:7–12, 14–18   Acts 14:8–18

There is a line in Walter Kerr's review of the new Edward Albee play that is worth relaying to you. The line goes something like this: "We have got to walk on water or sink. That being the case, we shall have to grow gills." This is a fair description of the church's options in America today: namely, walk on water or sink. Since the church is not a dependable walker on water and will therefore sink, its special, high-priority program should be the growing of gills with which to survive in the murky green underwater depths. The question is what will a church with gills look like.

The backlash is on and it is big. It cannot be reasoned

In the summer of 1966 the Chicago Freedom Movement, a coalition of S.C.L.C. and C.C.C.O. (the Coordinating Council of Community Organizations), led a number of marches into white communities to dramatize the segregated housing patterns in Chicago. The impact of this summer "movement" has been debated. There are those who feel that it served to weaken the growth of indigenous black community organizations and also served as a catalyst to strengthen the organization of the white backlash. The clergy and laymen who were in the streets in the summer seemed to disappear in the fall.

away, diminished in any of its fury by clever analysis. The church played a leadership role in representing the just claims of Negro people on the conscience of the country. The country seemed to respect this leadership, and its conscience was touched somewhat. But that has now changed. The country has begun chanting White Power, or had you noticed? The country's heartstrings are no longer available for plucking. All reckless defiance of law and order, of the stated authorities, and especially of the police can no longer be countenanced. There was a time when the presence of clergymen on picket lines and in protest marches gave dignity and moral stature to the event. That time has passed. Their presence today merely indicates to the populace that the church has sold out to all of the low-living minorities, the nonwhite minorities, and especially the Negro minority. Sold out. The presence of clergymen increases wrath and diminishes moral stature. The people of the country want *their* church back. They want their church back off the streets, back in the safety of doctrinal discussion. They want their pastors in offices where they can do pastoral counseling and parish visitation. And it looks like what the people want they are going to get. I say this because I have noticed a distinct shriveling of the radical core. Fewer and fewer men, at least in our Presbytery, are now (since July) willing to assign themselves a place in any activity that will attract backlash, since they serve primarily in backlash-type parishes. It is not news to you, either, that the national denominational boards and agencies are in a financial bind because backlash funds are being withheld. They are feeling the weight of the dissatisfaction of the people for the timid part they played in the brief so-called civil rights outburst. Receipts are way down this year. Just when certain hard-hit parishes need emergency money, the emergency money dried up. The church as an American institution consisting of all denominations and all persuasions, you see, no longer commands an audience or is persuasive in changing opinion. That is why I said: either walk on water or sink. And that is why I said, furthermore, that the only practical thing to do as an adaptive response to the total situation is to grow gills. And having done that, then . . . what? What is going to be the church's response to the backlash? A back backlash? Or silence on the issues that provoked the backlash? A vivid reassertion of what we once claimed to be the divine Word on racial justice or a new word that asserts what the backlash wants to hear?

We are now ready to attend to the scriptures. Both lections. Jeremiah was in danger, he says, of losing his life. While his fellow prophets were dealing in issues of personal morality and following the *Reader's Digest* line on foreign policy, i.e., we are good safe members of the Judah *team*, Jeremiah had been raising foreign policy issues exclusively. Jeremiah had been declaring boldly—with *élan* and a real flair—the courses Judah could follow, pronouncing without any equivocation that Judah and blessed Jerusalem were going to be occupied by the troops of a mammoth enemy army and that the citizens were going to perish by the sword or go into exile. Every one. This was not a popular word, as you can well imagine. Jeremiah had been imprisoned for his activity. He had been conspired against for his birthrighted land. He had been badly used by the king and his counselors. The city of Jerusalem seethed with hostility against him. Even his familiar friends denounced him. Considering these consequences, Jeremiah decided not to speak the Word of God any more. But then, as you heard in the reading, Jeremiah goes on: "If I say, 'I will not mention him, or speak any more in his name,' there is in my heart as it were a burning fire shut up in my bones, and I am weary with holding it in, and I cannot." The point of this is plain. Jeremiah has to deal with a relentless divine adversary if he refuses to deliver the Word of God. Like a burning fire shut up in his bones, he says. That to Jeremiah is worse than facing all the insults, prison, and desolation Jerusalem can muster. But I want you to see Jeremiah trying to find a way out. I want you to see Jeremiah keeping the living Word of God bottled up inside himself. Playing it safe and cosy. Trying to win his way back into the affections of his familiar friends. Getting back on good terms with his family, his teachers. Beginning to go to parties again. Refloated as an O.K. reformed prophet. You know, structurally the problem of a patient in a mental health facility returning back home. The patient has got to affect a super normality to reassure friends and family that all is again all right. This is what Jeremiah *wanted* to do. It would have been a great day for Jeremiah if only God had chosen another prophet and let Jeremiah go free. He preferred not being a prophet. And the reason I make this situation clear is to stop you from making a hero of Jeremiah whereby you can say he was special, he was hot stuff, he doesn't apply. He does apply. He applies as directly as Paul and Barnabas did to the citizens of Lystra. Notice that the citizens of Lystra attempted to wiggle out of the force of the good news spoken and enacted in their midst. They tried to make out that Paul and Barnabas were some kind of gods. It is within the province of gods, after all, to give the power to walk to hopeless cripples, is it not? Paul and Barnabas had a difficult time refusing the sacrifices. The people were that eager to get off the hook, return to normal, be done with momentary excesses of mystery and ecstasy. No more, however, can we in our backlashed circumstances flounce Jeremiah up to look like a hero, a next-to-God, when he was composed of the same cowardly stuff we are composed of, a lover of ease, good cigars, delightful conversation about Swinburne or Bergson, and a lover of no tension who positively hated having to take himself to the streets, there to sound the clear Word of God. He *had* to be a prophet. So do we. And if we have any quarrel, let us quarrel with God.

The situation is that you could not get people to come to a civil rights rally if you raffled a Cadillac on the side in Woodlawn, Chatham, Hyde Park, or any place to the north or far south. All of that exciting talk about Freedom Now and not being turned around and Michael rowing his boat ashore (a hybrid peacenik-racenik song) and We Shall Overcome is over. A prominent high school uses the "We Shall Overcome" tune for a football pep song now. Mr. Dirksen was pleased to honor his obligations to his vociferous constituents and thereby kill that poor weak little civil rights bill before the current Congress. *Northern* congressional candidates in Chicago are making out-and-out racist statements these days in order to get elected. The coalition of civil rights groups has fallen apart, and I believe—although it is hotly disputed—I believe the civil rights coalition is dead, and dead not because of Stokely Carmichael and Floyd McKissick but because the dominant white liberal support has dropped out. America understands money and the power of money and thus knows that the institutional civil rights movement can be killed by drying up its source of cash. Other institutions, such as the church, can be penalized for their civil rights activity by withdrawing funds. In a final showdown, the church might yet feel the power of a financial crusher and, too, die.

Does this strong American reaction to civil rights activity mean that the contentions of the movement were wrong? Are we to believe that all of a sudden the issue of constitutionally guaranteed freedom for minority citizens is no longer an issue? Are we to say that the evils of segregated education, the inequality of educational opportunity, are no longer evil—just because a backlash has occurred? When as late as July, the movement contended that gradualism is another name for never, has gradualism in October taken on some new philosophical force or gained some strength it once did not possess? Have the poor become less a cause of national scandal? Have the beaten and maimed ceased to claim compassion? You might think so, the way major churchmen, major specific churches, whole denominations, and numberless smaller local churches have all of a sudden, since July, backed away and have begun re-evaluating their stance. Have suddenly begun preaching about love and baptism and justification by faith and re-assuringly Biblical things, and not mentioning the also Biblical demands or the Bible's primary demand for justice?

A great vacuum exists. No one is now articulating the concerns and the immense injustices suffered daily by the Negro community in Chicago. All we are hearing is white power and George Wallace and backlash. And were some-one to stand in this tense situation to articulate the historic and legitimate demands of the Negro people, America would say, "We've heard it. We once heard and believed it. But we've heard it. Sit down." Not only, therefore, has a vacuum been created in the city's public discourse, a vacuum has been discovered to exist in the hearts and rhetoric of the strongest civil rights powers. Mr. Car-michael and Mr. McKissick are playing the same tunes and essentially the same words now to the black, self-con-sciously black community instead of to the white liberal coalitions of yesterday.

The time and place are, therefore, clear. Now. Here. The time, now, and the place, here, have been set to begin anew the prophetic task of awakening America to the prospect of its doom, an apocalypse of violence unless it makes clear its determination to accord to all citizens equally the possibility of constitutional democracy. Doom. Do great countries somehow secure exemptions from the demands of simple justice? No. By the great Word of God, no. Great countries perish. Die of internal discord, die self-inflicted deaths. This is the burden of the Word of God to America which the church must take on its lips, risking thereby further penalties in loss of prestige, money, and power.

As you think of this terrible thing, this loss of credibility and friends in the world, please think of the yet more terrible option. Consider South Africa. Let the example of South Africa sink in. It is founded on apartheid and lives in bad faith as an exemplar to the world of its determination to quash the humanity of black natives to whom, really, that rich land belongs. "But we do not practice apartheid," I heard you say. "Only segregation. In another hundred years," I hear you say. There is no difference. As surely as South Africa is doomed, the U.S. is, too. And its churches. So what is a little loss of credibility and friends?

But, not so serious, please. As we meet the claims laid upon us today, remember where the claims come from. We are not the saviors of the world. Jesus is. The worrying is his department. The action is ours. In doing we find not only responsibility and high moral fervor but also fun, good humor, ease, in a word, Grace. Is it not a gracious Word that gives us our very lives? Amen.

10

SHAME

DEUTERONOMY 26:1–11   MARK 8:27 to 9:1

I have been hearing all week long about the new Chicago sculpture on the plaza in front of the Civic Center building. And have been amused at the Mayor's determination to have Picasso's gift to Chicago well honored. Now he has got a winner, to begin with, and can hardly go wrong, and so far has had to rebut only people who declare that the sculpture is a baboon or a free-form junk heap. He has shown he will defend this gift, which started up a wild fantasy on my part. What if, the fantasy goes, what if some major critic, like the art critic for the *New York Times*—yes, what if Mr. John Canaday were to say that he knows exactly what the sculpture means because he knows Picasso, and Picasso told him directly what it means. What if Canaday said that Picasso told him that it was a big put-down to Chicago. That statue, says Picasso, reported by Canaday, does not represent a dog, lady, or baboon. That statue represents . . . hold your breath . . . BLACK POWER. PICASSO DIGS STOKELY would be the headline. Well, in this fantasy of mine, the major art critic, than which there is no more (or square), says "black power." Then in about fifteen minutes a squad would be out there on that plaza with cutting torches, cutting

113

up that lovely sculpture. Down it would come, instant rust and all, the Mayor declaring in his most purple manner that "the people of Chicago are a brotherly people who do not have time for this black power mischief." Now, I am not saying that is what the Picasso means. *Only* a fantasy.

I *am* saying that black power is an expression of great power; it awakens and quickens hope in most of us; it produces anger verging toward apoplexy in mayors, real estate boards, police departments, and, now, the F.B.I. Black power is vivid without being precise. No one knows exactly what it means, because it means different things to various people. That is its glory. It was first articulated in the deep South as an expression of frustration and rage over the lamentable disarray and sorry performance of the so-called civil rights movement, filled and dominated as it was by sandaled whites. Black power was first uttered in the deep southern situation of near total political impotence. It was intended to galvanize the black people of the South into full use of their political power. With absolute majorities in most counties, and decisive blocs in the remaining counties, black power advocates were saying that the political voice of black people could hereafter be *the* voice in electing officials. And, as if they had said more than they knew, their minds working fast, the black power advocates began to say that political power is a legitimate, democratically approved way to secure economic and social power. To be sure, most people in America—that is, mainstream American people, the people who look at Lady Clairol ads advocating becoming blondes without laughing—most American people secure economic and social power first, then parlay this power into political advantage. But black power advocates saw lots of Americans who were nothing until they got into politics (like L.B.J.), and so it is a viable, approved way of making democracy function for this large black minority.

I want to underline the simple origins of the expression "black power." It should have died four or five weeks later, like any decent slogan. That is the normal life of slogans. It should have suffered the fate of the bright things we carry around on bumper stickers ("Mary Poppins is a junkie"; "Stamp out mental health") and the bright things we say to each other at parties or laugh about on TV. But black power did not pass, because it was deeply evocative. I mean: it literally called things up. It quickened hope and hardened resolve. It was moderately successful even in its original setting. Julian Bond, one of the people who first started using the expression seriously and believing it, was, after all, elected to the Georgia legislature.

Black power seemed to spill over and grow and take on new meaning the more it was used, especially as its advocates took it north and east. One of the great things black power did was to take the lid off of being black. Yes. Black power did that singlehandedly. Until then there were, of course, lots of black people who were not unhappy over being black, and for whom being black was not a big personal problem. But it took this expression to produce a massive, positive, public appreciation of blackness, of naturally kinky hair. Afro-American enthusiasm in bright orange dresses. Yes. Ecstatic, *corporate* negritude. People enthusiastic about blackness. Rallies in Harlem that were the greatest yet. Snake-dancing marches. Excitement.

These were creative words uttered in a living situation to living people who responded instantly. These words did not continue to grow in meaning and expressiveness because more and more people began to use them. Because they got on national TV. Because *Time* magazine got wind of them and wrote out some cute remarks. No. These developments ordinarily kill the meaning and expressiveness of words. Black power grew and continues to grow at this minute in meaning and expressiveness because the people who use the term and understand it are growing. The users become more hopeful, more sophisticated, more *powerful* as the expression grows. Under the black power banner right now you have a very wide assortment of points of view, for instance. There is on the one hand the utterly benign and tranquil Dr. Nathan Wright, a black Episcopal clergyman who is talking about the "interpersonal requirements for true dialogic community." Clearly, Dr. Wright is a hundred-proof egghead, bonded eight years in Harvard. And under the same black power banner, on the other hand, you have Rap Brown, who is rather more . . . incendiary, in favor of conflict as the means best suited to galvanize black people into arrangements expressing black power where it really is: in major metropolitan areas and in the heavy concentrations of black people in the South. He commutes between Harlem and Baton Rouge. Now I heard the governor of Florida put Rap Brown down on an ABC news show; in fact, I have been impressed by the numbers of very big people who have lately been trying to put him down, discredit him, do him in, including the F.B.I. The more I see of this the more convinced I become that, for all his incendiarism, Mr. Brown is articulating a vitally necessary ingredient of all the things black power means to black people. Between Wright and Brown there are the thousands of others who have their special angles: voting, opening the stubborn job market, separatism, housing, Vietnam, community organization. They present these special angles under the auspices of black power.

It is, you see, an amazingly creative combination of words. These are living words that live because people believe in them *and* because they produce rather violent reactions, too. You are well aware, I guess, of the motions being made by the Establishment to hang the rioting tag on black power. Ridiculous. The opposite is true. Riots have been conducted by people who do not have power or the hope of power and who are just plain fed up. Riots are the expressions of the absence of black power; that is, of black powerlessness before the complex forces generated by white power in major metropolitan areas: the police, the courts, jobs, political machines, decrepit housing, the welfare apparatus, commercial gouging, schools, and the absence of recreation facilities. Nowhere to turn; no relief from this grinding, oppressive powerlessness. One tipping incident and . . . whoosh . . . the powerlessness explodes into violent, flaming, angry expression. For grown men to blame black power for the riots is cynical. Not infantile. *Cynical.* This failure to assess the agonies endured by black people, and the need to seek out a scapegoat, makes the incendiarism of Rap Brown more accessible than it ordinarily would be. And I was not altogether funning around when I said Daley would chop up the Picasso if he became convinced that it stood for black power. He would. Black power angers him. To him it means unrest, violence, riots, conflagrations. Above all, it means the end of machine control over predictable River Ward majority votes in black areas of Chicago. It means the end of his dominion over the black people of Chicago. He is half right. Black power does mean part of what he thinks it does. But his general angry perception of the creative energies being called up and put together by black power is an index, of sorts, of the power now actually being exercised by black people. He is worried, the man is. And that is good.

You know, I have been startled during the last month at congressional reaction to Newark and Detroit. I have been startled first at the representatives of the riot areas, who have not been black themselves and who have expressed the "angry beast" point of view. I have been startled next at the sun-clear fact that these people in the riot areas do not have representatives. Their ostensible representatives actually represent the adjacent areas and their bitter, uncomprehending points of view. Does that say anything to you? Let it sink in. Let it stew. Especially let it open up what is happening right here, among us, in Woodlawn and on the central South Side. Do you know that we are going to have a congressional election next spring and that, as political reality now shapes itself, it is going to be an inevitable contest between two white men, neither one of whom we could trust to stand up and tell it the way it really is if trouble were to break out here?

It has occurred to me that almost any black man would be preferable to the people now being lined up by the regular Democratic party. And it also pleases me to think that there is a certain black man who has political and intellectual endowments superior to the white men and who in every way manifests hopefulness, political savvy, and continuing identification with the black poor: namely, our rookie State Senator from the Twenty-fourth District, our friend and colleague. The name is Richard Newhouse. It is not too early (in fact almost too late) to begin considering the race in the First Congressional District and to begin considering the luxury of having Richard Newhouse in the Congress of the United States.

Which is what black power is all about. These words are living words that grow and change and inspire and enthuse and galvanize and upset and probe and reach out and touch the living tissues of historical as well as personal existence. Exactly like words once heard and used that we remember as Biblical words. Now, you would probably not guess from the way the words of Jesus are handled, gossiped about, distorted by thousands of us preachers and teachers, hashed up, chopped up, misunderstood, and misquoted that these were *once* living words of enormously generative power. You would never guess from looking at all the sleeping congregations of Christian folk in the land, waiting for the jokes in the sermons, dozing off, bored stiff—sequestered congregations, spilling over with elegance and affluence—that the words of Jesus about serving and being with the poor; about loving the neighbor, making peace with the brother; about loving the enemy, the stranger, the outcast . . . that these words once were like flames, that they produced unforgettable impressions and created communities. No, you would never guess it. Because the occasion for the words—that is, the belief, the responses, the yearnings, the livid authoritative example—are no longer present. These words of Jesus are like the dead rose leaves often stored in the Bible; they tend to flake and crumble to dust if handled at all.

The trouble the Christian church in America is in today springs from the lack of a context in which living words have any meaning. A church shaped by mottoes, by slogans, by propaganda, by cheap moralizing (producing guilt, unbelief, rage, and sterile conformity) is not a living church. A church which believes in itself first of all, its continuing viability, its own institutional existence, hoarding its treasure, *uses* the words of Jesus as a propaganda backdrop for programs it wants support for, programs, by the way, generally disdainful of humanity. The context is not only uncongenial to the livingness of the words of Jesus, it is a hostile environment antithetical to the livingness of these words. And this gives us, I should hope, some measure of insight into the New Testament lection, read for our blessing and advantage but a few minutes ago. "Whoever is ashamed of me and of my words in this adulterous and sinful generation, of him will the Son of man also be ashamed, when he comes in the glory of his Father with the holy angels." "Ashamed" is the word here. Of no account. As though this loyalty to Jesus and his words must be disclaimed, repudiated. To think of this previous loyalty brings *shame*, guilt, self-reproach. The writer of these words was writing during a time when the early ardor of the church had begun to cool: when the living context was emerging persecution; when the church was almost directionless, torn by factions, and in a quandary. Yes, shame is the adequate word. Thus the writer of this gospel has Jesus say, "Whoever is ashamed of me and my words in this adulterous and evil generation, of him will the Son of man also be ashamed."

Now, please, I am calling attention to the livingness of living words, which are accorded serious attention because they have indigenous power. And I am also calling attention how words die and, when remembered, produce shame. Not personal shame but existential shame: repudiation, that is. So I am saying (a) the words of Jesus are dead to us and (b) they are dead to us because we are in a context in which they cannot live. The words of Jesus are dead in such a way that they will not gain life by pumping in a lot of relevance, or by showing how like 1967 they are, or by making artful paraphrases. They do not change. They are there in the Bible. They are very old. Very, *very* old. But they are dead because we are in and have helped to invent a repudiating context governed by assumptions that are strikingly identical to those shared by the American dream, and flat-out free-enterprise capitalism, which is to say . . . WHITE POWER.

In our innocence (or ignorance) of the ways of God, we could well be a little sad over the deadness of dead words *or* castigate somebody, the laity or the clergy, for this deplorable state of affairs. But God is not "our" God, and he conforms to no norms and is creative beyond our knowing. He has not been on vacation since Pentecost. He is the living God, whose Word is still a living Word spoken in living situations to bring about the deliverance of the captive and health to the peoples of the earth. Only our extraordinary arrogance would assume that God's Word is dead because we have been ashamed of the words of Jesus. With any kind of sensitivity at all, any kind of faithfulness, we would be hearing the living words of our day, black power, *and* also the fabulously romantic words of the peacenik young, "Make love, not war," as the living words of the Lord and in that risk perhaps avert the shame that otherwise would be our due from the side of God for having repudiated our Lord and *his* words. It is the task of God to be creative, you know; it is the task of the church to be sensitive and faithful in heeding his every word. No matter if the whole world seeks to discredit black power, let us treasure these words as God's words to us . . . right now. Amen.

11

JESTING

This feast of detail. The names. Eglon the Moabite. Ehud the Benjaminite. A left-handed man. Was being left-handed so unusual that a left-handed man was a sort of freak? And what the left-handed Ehud did. Cunning. He made a commando knife. A long thin knife with two sharp edges. Because he might need it sometime? No. Because he liked to fool around at the blacksmith's? No. He had a plan, that's why. A program. And in the immortal words of Elder L. D. Jones, if you've got a program the people are going to come out. Ehud's plan was so simple, so easy of execution, so foolproof that it had to work. And the key to the success of the program was the psychological nomenclature of Eglon, the enemy king. Tribute. Bring money. That is what vassals had to do, what people in occupied lands have always had to do. Maybe all of these oriental-type monarchs were so vain that they always personally received the tribute and counted it themselves, not leaving it to their generals and secretaries of the treasury. But this was Eglon's style for sure. This was the pay-off and he enjoyed that. He enjoyed seeing the money coming to him. The formalities of the occasion, all of that long-winded nonsense where the enemy says his speech of how good Eglon is, how fair, and wishes Eglon good health, and Eglon reciprocating with a speech of reception full of lush material. The formalities of the occasion were: the subdued enemy should acknowledge in the most subtle possible way that Eglon is a fine and just king who has the upper hand, while Eglon in response must be all magnanimity, trying to mask the fact of his actual superiority in the situation by making the acceptance of the tribute appear to be a business deal. Well, of course. This was the pay-off. You better believe that Eglon would be right down there counting the tribute himself, and Ehud thus had an infallible plan: to send his escort away. What is this? A signal, as modern war systems planners say. We are always wanting to make sure that we are giving clear signals to Hanoi. An act that the enemy will recognize the full import of. But without saying so.

Send the escort away. What does this mean? That Ehud wants to talk to Eglon about a deal of some kind. Wants to connive. Something that it will be to Eglon's advantage to listen to. Who is Eglon? He is Sidney Greenstreet. He is A. J. Liebling. He is Fats Domino. He is a practical eunuch because of his bulk and thus extraordinarily interested in details, in conniving, in plotting, and sensitive to the possibility. As soon as the left big toe of the first escort begins to twitch before he turns to go, Eglon has the signal. He looks up . . . they go . . . ah . . . and Ehud in short order is by himself with Eglon, the talk for a bit confirming and reconfirming the fact that Ehud has something to propose, talking in those thundering formal flourishes that are the stock in trade of diplomats. Well, you see, you can't just out and say anything. You can't just threaten or promise or wheedle until you have investigated the climate of acceptance on the other side of the table, and the other side is earnestly probing you to find out what you have in mind before indicating whether the climate will in fact be acceptable. That is what diplomacy is all about. That is what Ehud and Eglon did: sparred, jockeyed for position; and when it appeared that they could in fact do business they arranged to put the deal into words. A private meeting between heads of state. The fat man caught alone in a trap of his own devising: namely, his love for deals and counterdeals. Eglon has already canvassed in his own mind every conceivable angle. He has thought of every proposal that Ehud can make and has plotted in his own mind his response to each of Ehud's potential proposals. Just as the U.S. and U.S.S.R. and the Peoples' Republic of China do even to this day. And it never occurred to Eglon that Ehud had murder on his mind. How did Ehud know that? Well, Ehud *did* know that Eglon would not expect a personal attack. And so that commando knife. Strapped there to his right leg under his britches. That commando knife made with such tender care, hammered out so carefully, tempered, sharpened, shined, oiled, and felt—yes, hefted, found out. Ehud had found out about that knife all the time he was making it, had been testing his plan. That is why he did not go over to E. J. Korvette's and buy one. He needed to *do* the plan and feel the knife grow in his hand so that the knife would at the appropriate time be a grown-out extension of his left hand. Practice. Did he ever practice the draw, the lightning draw, the lightning draw and thrust before Eglon ever knew that he was under attack, before even a hand would be raised to ward off the thrust? Yes, I dare say he practiced. He went through the whole scene 47,000 times. Ready. Ready for the cool roof chamber. Alone with the fat man. "I have a message from God for you." Eglon nodding, appreciatively, loving the moment of the deal but never to nod again; slumping over, fatally stabbed. Ehud, of course, escaped, roused his countrymen and his kinsmen, and they retook the vital fords of the Jordan River, repelled the Moabite counterattack, and were free of the hated Moabite dominion over their lives.

Just like Napoleon Solo, you say, or Batman. Superior equipment and planning will win every time. This is what the story seems to say part of the time, and the story seems to say that the real leaders of Israel between Moses and Saul were the doers who excelled in this inter-Semitic warfare of centuries-long duration, excelled precisely in achieving victory, local hard-won victory, over a foe who would have to be put down again another time. All of these people who thought that their living space was constricted, pushing and shoving and elbowing each other around. Borders always being adjusted by the sword. Cities changing hands, and pasture lands. A terrific premium was placed on this cunning strength displayed by Ehud and Othniel and Shamgar.

But that is certainly not all that the story says. The writer introduces a theological interpretation. This is found in verse fifteen where the writer says, "But when the people of Israel cried to the Lord, the Lord raised up for them a deliverer, Ehud. . . ." Well, now that has all the marks of a kind of ritualistic theological formula. The varied material of Israel's history is being stuffed into these preset categories, especially the category of deliverance. But, of course, this is the only way an Israelite writes, can write: namely, with deliverance in his mind. Israel sees itself as a delivered people. It sees itself in this having-been-delivered relationship to God. The story of Ehud is an Old Testament analogue to the Easter story, and we are addressing ourselves to it this Sunday following Easter because it is an Easter story: deliverance. Deliverance was in the mind of its writer precisely as deliverance was in the minds of *all* the first-century writers. They both deal with deliverance and in essentially the same way.

Farthest from the mind of the writer is any kind of notion of *automatic* deliverance. There are the people in Egypt. God invents some 707 El Al Jets and whisks them all back home, not in forty years but in forty minutes. The people are paying tribute to Eglon. God takes pity on his people and sends some lightning down on Eglon. Not automatic at all. The people *walked* out of Egypt. They *seized* the fords of the Jordan and fought a furious battle. Ehud lived through every moment of creating his plan. The deliverance is real enough. The most fastidious historian would say, Yes, Eglon was killed and the Israelites seized the fords of the Jordan and threw back the Moabite army. He would say, The rest of it, the deliverance part—well, that is in the mind of the writer. Indeed it is. So much in the mind of the writer that this story is not remotely like the adventures of those fellows from U.N.C.L.E. It is more like the story somebody will write someday about the struggle that preoccupied the colored people of the U.S. during the latter half of the twentieth century. Now for a while in the early part of the struggle, there was in the minds of the people themselves an acute self-knowledge of going someplace. "Keep on walking toward the Freedom Land." No theatrics, no Napoleon Solo stuff at all. All of the people had to *get* together in their minds and hearts, *stay* together, *help* each other along, *do* for each other, and *keep* going on and on. There was this distinct accent on deliverance, being delivered, on walking on toward the Freedom Land: a deliberate theologically sound understanding of the movement in relationship to Israel's deliverance from Egypt. And now there is a kind of fumbling around and massive attempts to recreate circumstances to redo the tactics that proved so effective in the early years of the struggle.

Ehud has not yet arisen, or he is still making his knife or is practicing his fast draw. But the delivered people are crying once again for deliverance, and here is where we begin to plumb the depths of the theological point of view of the writer. His point of view is that God is not consistent, regular in his omnipotence. He is creative. He exercises his Lordship in majestic but also in daring and novel ways. Surprise is the principal mark of his appearance within the Old Testament structures. Surprise, yes, and a sort of arbitrariness. Not a general God, *pro forma* God, but a God in behalf of his people, a God who stays up nights figuring out what to do, and a determined God, divinely willful. Determined that his people walk in his way and, like him, become creative, surprising, novel, justice-loving, righteousness-adoring, peace-seeking. So that when Ehud is there at the forge—well, God has once more delivered his people. The fact of Ehud's hands operating the forge announces the ultimate victory.

Now this is definitely a theological structuring of events, twenty-twenty hindsight. The theological *historian* is saying that when Ehud was working at the forge the Moabites were already defeated. He was not alive, of course, when it happened, and when it did happen there was no one around to whisper, "Look at that Ehud, ain't he somethin'? He's going' after Eglon next week." And so it appears, when viewed within rigorously applied rational canons, that whenever a victory occurs the theological historian will come along and claim the victory for God when it really belongs to Ehud.

But we are not talking about rigorously applied rational canons. Here is some light upon our way. The Hebrews believed that something was going to happen. They knew something was going to happen and they knew that Yahweh their God was at the bottom of it, provoking it. Creatively provoking creativity; which is to say, delivering his people. And inseparable to the deliverance was the ironlike belief that the deliverance was coming. The theological historian did not make up this belief and insert it backwards into the period. He was experiencing what it was to be a Hebrew.

Now I find the same thing today in the freedom struggle. Run into a cooled-off period. City Hall has learned how to react, has adjusted its responses so that it can cope with those old tactics. Is the struggle over? Ha! Never believe it. There is an unshakable certitude among us that there is some Ehud somewhere walking back and forth, his mind working around, turning it over, this plan, this way to do it, his whole being and the being of a whole people concentrated in this beginning of a plan. It is this way with him right now. Perhaps he is refining the plan, taking the kinks out, working, worrying, and, if he is anything like Ehud, and he is, then he is probably chuckling with mad, divinely inspired laughter at how simple, how ridiculous, how perfect the plan is. How surprising.

Leszek Kolakowski, an outstanding Polish intellectual, has written a brilliant, amazing philosophic essay entitled "The Priest and the Jester." In the essay he discusses thoroughly the absolutist and the dialectically questioning stands of philosophic thought and intellectual activity. He then ends the essay by noting that the priest has to be a finalist. He elaborates the doctrines of certitude, that which is unshakable, absolutely true. He holds together the traditions by sanctifying them with doctrinal finality, whereas the Jester takes nothing for granted, questions everything final, absolute, certain, because he believes passionately that truth is not a final metaphysical entity out there but a dialectical stopping point right now. So with Socrates, for instance, whose questioning patriotism was unquestioned, thus entitling him to death at the hands of the unquestioning Establishment patriots whose patriotism was so questionable.

This distinction has weighty consequences. It has often been remarked, and needs saying here again, that in original sit-ins the kids just did it. Jesters, you see. It was not written in the Bible that they cannot get hamburgers and Cokes at the same public drugstore where they can buy aspirin. So they sat in and were summarily thrown in jail. Well, the mothers were worried and went flying down to jail and phoned up their pastors, and then they came down and the TV came, and who should turn around as the spokesmen for the movement? The last ones there, the pastors.

This Old Testament reminiscence lines up with the Jester-Priest division of duties. The Jester acts, the Priest then finalizes, and both are illuminated mightily by the figure of Ehud enigmatically working away on his knife.

Freedom, yes, there's going to be freedom because God has such partiality for the Jester and creates a sufficient number to keep the earth from grinding to an ice-bound halt. Amen.

12

SOUL

GENESIS 2:4b–9   LUKE 12:13–21

"Beware of all covetousness, for a man's life does not consist in the abundance of his possessions." To covet is to want something someone else has and to want it because he has it . . . first. At the beginning there does not seem to be much here to worry us today. We may believe that we have the coveting front pretty well covered. And, anyway, of all the sins this seems the least exciting or dangerous. Coveting is not a thing we wake up worrying about whether we have it; it is a pretty innocent little diversion and certainly not one of your really big-time sins. The point is, however: beware of all covetousness; and to indicate that it is a treacherous, slippery, and cunning reality, Jesus told a parable. As we shall shortly see, it is not a clear story. It is puzzling, in keeping with covetousness.

The story goes this way: "The land of a rich man brought forth plentifully." So it is a rich man we are talking about, who does not have to worry about the electricity being turned off or how to keep the bailiff out. This rich man had a great crop. The rain came at the right time. The summer heat came at the right time. No insect raids or infesting worms. Just a fine bumper crop. The rich man thought to himself: "What shall I do, for I have nowhere to store my crops?" A fine kind of problem to have: more crops than barns to put them in. The reverse of the problem most farmers have most years: more barns than crops. The rich man thinks to himself some more: "I will do this: I will pull down my barns, and build larger ones"—great big ones, and paint them red and sell advertising on them to Bull Durham or Days Work—"and there I will store all my grain and my goods." Biggest barns in the county. Prettiest barns, too. Have some place to keep all my equipment besides lying around under some dinky little sheds. All work out fine. "And I will say to my soul. Soul, you have ample goods laid up for many years; take your ease, eat, drink, be merry." What happened to this man? God said to him: "Fool! This night your soul is required of you; and the things you have prepared, whose will they be?" And Jesus concluded the story with this terse comment: "So is he who lays up treasure for himself, and is not rich toward God."

I think instantly of the Presbyterian church in the years following the war until 1960 as I hear this story. Just like the rich man in the story, the Presbyterian church was really having bumper crops. Every year the denomination grew. Sunday schools grew. Youth groups grew. Women's associations grew. Why, they were having two services on Sunday mornings to keep up with the people, and when they got too many people they tore down their barns and built bigger and fancier barns and often these bigger barns were full of dedication. And where were all of these people coming from? First Church, for one place, and Sixth Church and Hope Church and Second Church, and Seventh Church and from no churches at all, just from the city, out of the city, away from the concrete and onto the grass. Split-level havens from air pollution, water pollution, lousy schools, havens from you know who . . . THE problem. This was a time of unparalleled prosperity. Good times.

Fire and Blackstone

Very few people in those days were willing to see that the church was profiting from an exodus out of the city which was going to have disastrous consequences. Nobody could predict a summer like '67, much less '68, during those days. The people just kept coming, and the church just kept growing and building and eating . . . family night dinners . . . and drinking . . . gallons of coffee . . . and being merry, as only the well fixed can be merry. The Presbyterian church happily assumed the task of being chaplain to a white fortress and willingly—willingly? *happily*—undertook the task of preparing new generations of white power to run America. Yes, the church did this without raising a question. The church was glad to. *Now,* of course, the general racist intent of that exodus is clear. *Now* we know what is meant by family churches, *now* we know what people mean when they say Sunday school. But the Presbyterian church did not know then. It was not bewaring of covetousness and so lost its soul; it did not give a hang about covetousness. It cared about the bigger barns and bigger budgets and two services plus hot and cold running pastors all over the place, in Christian Education buildings big enough to give the Christian Education directors something to work with, training children in the subtle dialectics of injustice. Because it was not bewaring of covetousness and because it lost its soul, it wonders why it cannot respond to the national crisis now with anything but the noise of a hawk or some blatherings about reconciliation.

Have *you* been noticing what Jesus has been saying in this story? Have you been hearing what *word* he is using and *how* he is using it? Did you maybe for a second think you were at 47th and Langley? Do we dare believe that he—well, "knew" about . . . Soul? I think we had better not believe that he knows about what is now known as the Soul. Not the same way.

Look: the way you know Soul is the way the Bible knows Soul. For the last thirty years now, theologians and Biblical scholars have been saying over and over again that Soul is not a separate compartment of a person, different from his body. They have been saying the Soul is not the immortal part while the body is the mortal part. Let me read some technical stuff that was written fifty years ago.

The Israelitic conception of man is made clear to us through the myth of creation; even though the latter is adopted from other nations, it still preserves the stamp of the Israelitic manner of thinking. Like the Egyptians' God Chhum, Yahweh, as a potter, moulded man of clay or earth, and into the moulded image he breathed his breath, in which manner man became a living soul. It is not the object of the narrator to analyze the elements of man, but to represent his essential character. The basis of its essence was the fragile corporeal substance, but by the breath of God it was transformed and became a *nephesh*, a soul. It is not said that man was supplied with a nephesh, and so the relation between body and soul is quite different from what it is to us. Such as he is, man, in his total essence, is a soul. . . .

All sensations act together in the making of the mental image. To the soul of a man pertain his appearance, his voice, the more or less hairy quality of his skin, his smell. To this must be added his manner of acting, all that he has done, all that belongs to him, which elements together constitute his soul. Among all the impressions received of him continuity obtains, the one immediately calling forth all the others, and of course, first and foremost, those which stamp the essence of his being with its special characteristics.*

Nephesh . . . living totality . . . Soul. The totality of man as he actually is. You see, exactly, what Soul means now. Soul doesn't come from any place. Can't be bought

* *Johannes Pedersen*, Israel *(London: Oxford, 1954, photo reprint).*

in the store. Can't be imitated, especially when someone says, five years too late, "Well, isn't that something else." That is bought Soul. Old Soul. Fake Soul and no Soul at all. Soul is the man and not a part of him or an affectation or a cultural development. Soul is the man doing and being who he is: fully, grandly, openly, without reservation or apology.

What thirty years of concentrated theological teaching could not do, the upsurge in black consciousness has accomplished in a matter of five or six years. Soul has become a real word again that really can be used and that makes possible the real hearing of this story told by Jesus. The man lost his Soul, and to lose Soul is to lose more than *everything*—to lose Soul is worse than being stomped and slaughtered, worse than dying so that whether dead or alive it is better to be dead. There is no more totality. No more human grandeur. What's left? A measly heap of possessions . . . things . . . junk.

Well, what did this man in Jesus' story do wrong? When you go over the story, you can hardly find what he did wrong. He acted sensibly. He made bigger barns because of his huge crop. He cannot be faulted there. Was he going to leave the stuff out in the fields and let it rot? He protected his overage, and when it was done, he planned to take his ease and celebrate a little. What did he do wrong? Since there appear to be no good answers to the question, maybe the question is wrong. Maybe we want to know, plainly, what did he do wrong, so that what he did wrong we can avoid doing and thus escape what happened to him. Not much Soul in the question? A pretty *square* question, really; no style; no subtlety; no feeling for the totality of a man, as though he does something at five some afternoon and at five after five something terrible happens. Of course, but maybe something inside the man went rotten. Not all of a sudden . . . boom . . . he is rotten; but subtly, slowly, no boom at all, but rotten inside, none the less. So that he grew hard where he should be soft, *in* his heart, and grew cruel, unbending, hardhearted. Then grew soft when he should have been hard, in his hands and his belly from his taking his ease. Maybe his eyes stopped laughing and became beady, calculating, mean eyes. Maybe his walk turned out wrong. No longer straight up and brimming and full of who he was. He started walking like he was in a hurry, with no inner music to measure his steps, hurrying even if he was not in a hurry. Maybe the suits he bought, even if he paid $200 cash, were wrong . . . no Soul. Whatever he did expressed the true condition of the man: he had lost his Soul. Whatever he *had* expressed . . . no Soul. Whatever he *did* expressed . . . no Soul. He *had* no Soul.

No, we are not going to find out here, one, two, three, what he did wrong so that we can cunningly avoid the wrong and thus avert the loss. The very fact that we would take that way maybe shows how little Soul is left among us, how little appreciation for the subtle totality of a man, his expressiveness, his complicity.

Soul is a gift, not an achievement; Soul is a being, not a doing. The only priceless gift, totally unrelated to price, wealth, barter, sale, things, goods. But as a gift Soul can be lost. Which to lose is to lose *more than* everything, to have lost even the capacity for knowing it has been lost. The man in tearing down his barns to build bigger, newer, better, prettier barns was displaying that he had lost his Soul. You see, he lost not only everything but lost the totality by which to understand that he had lost his Soul. He was no longer rich before God. God no longer looked out upon that man as he looks out upon all his creatures, shaking his head in delight at his creation. Isn't that what being rich toward God means? God looked out upon him and saw nothing, nobody. All God saw was treasure, barns, crops, tractors, equipment, paraphernalia; people getting treasure, loot, turning themselves into pirates as they went, smashing other people around, in order to get the loot. Pushed on by this desire to be even with someone else or up and beyond someone else. Robbing and murdering and stabbing people to get treasure, to get what someone else has. You think this isn't a big-time sin? You think they just added the Commandment against coveting so they could get an even number ten? No, sir. Soul gets obliterated, wiped out, smashed by desiring these things. Soul finds things to express itself, its beauty, its powers. Things were placed on this earth according to the Genesis myth of creation for the purpose of Souls. So that Souls could express themselves and fill themselves with what they need. For Souls to desire things merely because another Soul has them is to have begun an utterly inappropriate and distinctive course of action sure to end in the loss of Soul, which to lose is to have lost everything, even the capacity to understand that all has been lost.

We end where we began: Beware of all covetousness, this dangerously cunning enemy of Soul.

To this church: beware of all covetousness, beware of coveting the good old days, the good old full pews and overflowing offering plate and full Sunday schools and swanky people. Beware of coveting those outrageously full and opulent churches around you. Look neither to the left nor to the right with desire in your eyes, or else you will be tricked by one stronger than you and you will lose your . . . Soul.

To you personally: you want this and you want that with just and good reason because your Soul has need of them. Yes, and maybe you want to be free of one anxiety and needing and want to be free of a people which knows the constant enervating anxiety of needing.

You will want these things because other people apparently have them. Do not be deceived. God is not mocked. You will begin wanting those things so much and will do whatever is necessary to do to get them and stop wanting the main thing—free and glorious Soul—and lose your Soul.

Beware of all covetousness in order to continue to be rich toward God, who knows all about tyrants and will provide the means appropriate for the living of your Souls' lives. Amen.

13

COP-OUT

ECCLESIASTES 2:1–11; 4:1–3

In one Braniff Airlines commercial on TV there is an aging lady who takes advantage of Braniff's hospitality in the air. She takes table service, magazines, gum, and candy, and as she walks off the plane takes a blanket which she uses as a serape, then in the last shot hops up on the tractor and pulls the whole plane off. Now, I ask you: What is the function of such a commercial? Does it make claims that Braniff's hospitality as an airline is superior? I think not. If anything it tends to spoof notions of hospitality by portraying Braniff as an *easy* airline. Does it invite people to ride Braniff? Not in so many words. The invitation is made, all right, but in a circling sort of way. We are an airline big enough, bright enough, solid enough to use TV commercial time, which is notoriously expensive, in a kind of humorous way. We, too, are very big, very in. We paint our planes these pastel colors, and so on. So in this circling kind of way the TV audience is invited to fly on Braniff and why? Because Braniff has joined the numbers of TV advertisers who have given up first on the hard sell, then on the soft sell, and now use a no-sell technique, which for word-weary America is a relief. I invite your attention to this important development. Some commercials are more pleasing as entertainment than the shows they interrupt. Since I do not own color TV or even know what it looks like, I cannot get the full message, but in black and white, even, the photographic textures are superb, so much better than the standard low-budget series show. And some commercials have a gentle bite. Actual social commentary. Satire in commercials. Like the current series of Excedrin commercials in which the war between the sexes is the major motif, and not the superlative powers of Excedrin, which is only casually mentioned. And Alka-Seltzer, which was one of the pioneers in this field of entertaining commercials. In the Alka-Seltzer commercials the occasions for acid production in the stomach are highlighted. Such as the wife is going to take up driving, the husband forgets anniversary, and so on. This commercial assumes that excessive production of acid in the stomach is caused by excessive tensions. And that Alka-Seltzer was designed to handle this very modern situation in a very modern way. Among the gasolines, Clarke has a recurring motorist character whose '59 Chevrolet was restored from its rusty, bent, beat-up condition to a brand-new condition by the mere addition of Clarke's gasoline. This same motorist runs out of gasoline a mile or so from a station. The attendant unreels a mile-long hose to fill it up, except the car accidentally rolls away from motorist and attendant . . . rolls right into the Clarke station. Which is—well, listen . . . the commercial invited the audience to think that the motorist was a cluck. If the car rolled to the station, why didn't he coast the car in, instead of walking? And that is a long way from the old days when advertisers were afraid of their shadows when it came to calling motorists clucks, offending them. And in the present series, this same motorist, who wears big horn-rimmed glasses, is cleaning his engine. He has taken the whole thing apart and is cleaning it with soap and water, inside and out. The non-pitch is that Clarke's gasoline, you guessed it, does *the* job.

Well, well. Things are looking up in TV commercials. Schlitz commercials focus attention on the lengths that their people go to in order to secure Schlitz because it is so much better than just plain old beer. One man in the late night dresses over pajamas, goes out into a driving rainstorm, and returns because his wife mistakenly had purchased just any old beer and not Schlitz that day. In the Hamm's commercials, sky-blue water, which in the hard-sell days was Hamm's selling point, has become the occasion to introduce a cartoon character, a little bear, who is mostly fanciful but in a mildly amusing way. But the number-one commercial is the insurance commercial which asks, "Are you fully insured?" then unrolls a sequence to follow up the question. You see someone throwing a rock through your window, vandalizing your automobile; you see your house catch on fire and last you see this . . . man . . . walking into your living room. He trips on the rug, his feet go out, *all* the way out, from under him and as he falls to the floor his head hits the edge of your coffee table. Now these are grisly scenes done in a purposefully grisly way. So that you are helped to realize that this is a hearty joke and so when the man trips and falls you laugh, actually laugh out loud, especially when his head hits the table. Why? Because this is 1967, son. That's why. Because these very real catastrophes, when run together like paints, become a different color; you know, these catastrophes become . . . funny. And for a word-weary America, still drenched in hard-driving commercials, weekly propaganda broadcasts from Washington, communiqués from the New Politics Convention, exhausting analyses of why we are saving the lives of ten thousand American boys by bombing North Vietnam and

140

not seeding the Haiphong harbor with mines, for a people still hearing an awful lot of words, these pleasing, non-message-carrying ventures sponsored by advertisers are a great relief and also a sign of the times.

Please notice that thrift is seldom encountered as a reason for buying a specific product. Everybody knows about the generally equal price structure of competing products. So thrift is out. Please notice that sex is also out as a vehicle for securing audience approval of the product. Some years ago America was finding out about a trained psychologist who hired himself out to an advertising concern as a specialist in the field of man's hidden motivations, secret wishes; his basic drives. He thus made a fortune telling advertisers interesting things, such as: a man who buys a regular sedan is affirming his marriage relationship. A man who buys a convertible is affirming his desire for a mistress. And what did automobile people do with this solemn nonsense? They whisked right off to the drawing board and invented the hardtop, a compromise, you see, between sedan and convertible. For a while about everything, from Cat's Paw rubber heels to ant powder, was sold in the context of bosomy long-legged beauties dressed in very little. Please notice that this is gone. It has now been convincingly demonstrated that the boys from Vienna do not know very much about advertising.

More and more advertisers are using their time to develop these pleasing scenes, pleasing photographic textures using soft focus, low soft sound (semi-bossa-nova beat, quiet music plus flutes). More and more advertisers are trying to get the interest of word-weary America and in so doing are developing a vision of America as being filled with bright, pretty people, pleasantly dressed, unafflicted, happy, with oodles of leisure time, moderate, well-married, well-familied, and talented. All very young. (Except Mrs. Olson, who only gets in because she knows how to make coffee.) Electronic-turned-on, you see. Both wet and mild as per 7-Up and slim as per Diet Pepsi. The go generation. Beyond words. Beyond America's trouble—sensitive and sensuous. Marshall McLuhan points out in one of his observations that is accurate that these people are beyond hot sex, hot movies, hot books, and have cool sex, enjoy the cool medium (TV), and disdain books.

America is not like that, of course. Let's please keep our feet on the ground. Not all Americans own TV, and not all Americans who do own TV look at the thing. And more, America's troubles do not go away because someone yells "Surf's up!" We are being gulled by the advertisers, who have been responsible more than anyone else for the word weariness and who now seek to deliver us from that condition with gentle guitar music, deliver us not back to our previous sanity but into a new, glittering, highly segregated world of great plenty. The sign over the door to this new land is TROUBLE-FREE AMERICA. You will look in vain for riots here. Civil disorders. Agonies. Hunger. Dismal schools without textbooks, pencils, or toilet paper, or the two ladies who came into the offices of our Excluded Child Development Program ten days ago looking for some help, *any* help, in getting some place to live. Because where they had been living and paying hefty rents they did not dare go to sleep. So they had pooled their children, made them all sleep in one room along with one mother while the other mother guarded them against . . . rats. Can you imagine a rat in one of those Winston parties? or in a Right Guard commercial? Trouble-free. Only lower back pains, B.O., and bad breath. These are the only enemies in Trouble-free America. Did you know that people do not kiss if one or both has bad breath? Well, thanks be to God for Colgate 100, Micrin, Listerine, and Reef; there is no need to stop kissing because no need for bad breath up to twelve hours.

A whole wonderful world. A world of plenty: wines, fruits, breads, imported sardines, shining buildings, landscaped gardens, luscious purples, rich oranges, psychedelic swirling blues, limpid pools, and money; silvers, golds, the rich crinkling substantial lovely feel of . . . bonds. All that a heart can desire. But more than that, all that in previous, less productive times a king's heart could possibly desire. Now available for your purchase. Ready for occupancy now. Run right down to your. . . . Hurry out to your. . . .

Obviously, I think it important to recognize this newly created Trouble-free America, You-all. This cool and affluent world with long-legged blonde beauties parading around in their mini bikinis because that is what Milwaukee is all about. That is the meaning of those ominous confrontations in Chicago all summer: up so close to the flash point and then laughing retreats. Did you know that the Milwaukee Youth Council and the N.A.A.C.P. are seeking to engineer a nationwide selective buying campaign against Schlitz? And did you know that the speakers on 43rd Street at the wall criticize James Groppi for leading the Milwaukee campaign because he is a white man? And that these speakers are cheered?

Certainly we must not burst into vindictive criticism of these advertisers for having created a luscious Trouble-free America, because they could not have been successful unless escapist wishes were present in our hearts ready to be pandered to, and we probably ought not be vindictively critical of the escapist wishes which are the cornerstone of Trouble-free America. I call your attention to the most prominent motif: namely, the word weariness; to America's exhaustion with having heard so many words, so many slanted, cunning, lying words. I call your attention

to the fall of rhetoric, to any rhetoric. The rhetoric of
H. L. Hunt, the rhetoric of Stokely Carmichael. The
people are no longer persuadable. Mr. Ford fulminated
against the unions with dire warnings and examples of
intransigence. We yawned. We knew he would go to the
bargaining table, that his speech was a part of a rhetorical
minuet. Walter Reuther expressed the conviction that the
real issue in this strike was the dignity of the Ford worker.
We yawned and reached for the Fritos, because we knew
he would soon settle the thing at less than asked for.
Right? People do not believe in words or series of words,
in promises, in facts. Why, facts can turn into snow jobs
in the middle of summer. People do not believe words
without exception. You know, even words like Gospel,
America, Justice. That great word "justice" is no longer
an empowering word. It is not as exciting as Scotch, bra,
trip. When words do not reach into the being of people
who on hearing them tend to believe or not believe,
tend to be glad or angry, then act, rhetoric as such has
fallen. Any rhetoric: the rhetoric supporting the far right,
the rhetoric of the administration in drumming up support
for our foreign policy, the rhetoric of the left, the rhetoric
of revolutionaries, the rhetoric of ins, the rhetoric of preachers. What is this that I am speaking right now? Am I
coming at you with pictures? No. With words. Words
devised in special ways to appeal eventually to your sensibilities, to your outrage, but with spirited words in a
spoiled setting: namely, the pulpit. Only the antic Peter
de Vries can really picture how incongruous are the developed ways in which the professionally religious talk to
the amateur religious. And Mr. de Vries, the funny man's
funny man, sees the area of public discourse blighted as
much by the bad faith and manipulative efforts of the
preacher as by the indifferent sort of consumerism found
in the pews. Which now finally gets us to the point of

the sermon: What are we not going to do about this outrageous split in our land? Good Presbyterians that we are, we are going to attend to scripture.

With sparkling cynical wit the great Koheleth, the preacher so squarely named Ecclesiastes, this Koheleth examined approximately the same landscape we have just been over. He wrote up a little scenario about his attempts to overcome nausea by enjoying affluence. He did it so well that it could be printed in *Playboy* right now. Elegant stuff. You can just feel oozing affluence all over his prose. Until you read the comedown. Remember how it goes: "And whatever my eyes desired I did not keep from them; I kept my heart from no pleasure, for my heart found pleasure in all my toil, and this was my reward for all my toil." Devastating. It was the accumulation of stuff, after all, and not the pleasure from the stuff. The entrepreneur as hero. Playboy consumer man as hero. Not lover as hero, government as hero, rich-beyond-rich man as hero. But worker as hero! The affluence shows up as a fake, to start with. Trouble-free, easy, swill-it-up-at-the barbecue Americans, you-all, get their basic pleasure out of perceiving themselves at the barbecue. Therein lies the whole story.

And we move on. Koheleth then investigated the plight of the poor only to encounter these same people as in the first scenario oppressing the poor. The Trouble Free have managed it off of the trouble of the poor in an ever expanding, ever more vicious circle. What place have words against such invincible structures? What power have words against a desire for pleasure which is best satisfied by oppressing the poor, which is to say, by plain old Calvinist work?

So that is why we had better not go to the Lincoln Memorial again to reinvest the democratic mythology with fresh moral power. That is why we had better stop hoping that prejudice will be overcome by persuasion. And that is why all of the human words in the rhetoric of the Democratic Left can be so easily dismissed. Bombast. Ignorant of the cunning dynamisms of the enslaving over the slaves.

Koheleth, not Herman Kahn, invented the statement of a situation in which the living envy the dead. He called that the situation of being on the wrong end of a Trouble-free land. And considering with rational force all the possibilities, he ended with his choice, which was: not ever to have been born in the first place. And who really can quarrel with him who has been both places: at the helm of a thirty-seven-foot Chris-Craft beauty and up the rotted stairs and then into an apartment with ample rats and no furniture for eight people in three tiny rooms? Both places. Really there. Yes. It is better not ever to have been born.

Koheleth could not act on this possibility of not ever being born. He had already been born. So he articulated a stinging series of laments on the vanity of the haves oppressing so rigorously the have nots who have not because of the aggressive appetites of the haves. In order to be sure he is understood, that we understand he is not merely using a slippery new mode of social protest, beyond rhetoric somehow, he then doubled both and lamented the vanity of vanities. You know he could not possibly be more honest and crystal clear than that. You and I might want to improve on this very hard way to end. We are in fact directly tempted to feel a big surge of hope language coming on. But we would know, I think, that hope language functions, especially for the affluent among us, as the last masquerade for our acceptance of this whole bloody American scene. No. No. No. Rather the hard ending than an upbeat cop-out. Or, to say it in a way congenial to Koheleth: Better dead than said. Amen.

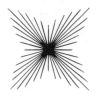

PART FOUR

The Church and Blackstone

14

THE CHURCH
AND BLACKSTONE

Let us be very frank at the beginning. The Session of
this church has made clear and unequivocal decisions that
sanction in general the formal programmatic relationship
between the church and the Blackstone Rangers. But there
have been many decisions I have made about particular
matters that the Session has not acted on and indeed may
not be fully acquainted with. I do not want to hide behind
the Session. And in this same spirit of recklessness, I want
to make it perfectly clear that the theological statement
I am about to make is not St. Paul's statement or John
Calvin's statement. It is my own statement, drawn up
last night. I hope the Session will support the statement.
I hope Harold Walker and the Ranger staff and you friends
and members of the congregation will support the state-

*In October, 1966, shortly after the distribution of "the Black
Paper" which described the relationship between First Presbyterian Church and the Blackstone Rangers, I spoke to the congregation on a Sunday evening, at which time I outlined four
basic principles which underlay my conception of the church's
involvement with the Rangers.*

ment, but let us be clear—it is mine. I am a fallible man who is prone to error. Quite possibly I am crazy. But at least as of now I am your pastor and as such am called to make theological statements.

I take it for granted that we understand the church to be a missionary agency for the world whose function is to give its life away. I consider it elementary and not needful of further discussion. The church is not a bank or a city agency or a religious club for any one class or people. The church is a center for human and humane activity, exactly following the model of humanity and humaneness that is found in Jesus, who in the church is confessed to be Lord. The church, therefore, is full of people whose eligibility has not been checked out at the door, full of people whose reputation need not be ascertained. The church is full of forgiven sinners, and its natural climate is grace. The church turns no one away. The church provides sanctuary to anyone. The church, furthermore, is helpful and generous. To me these matters are so basic that they do not need elaboration or defense. If we challenge these descriptions of the church, we challenge the Christian faith itself. So I take it for granted that we agree already on this fundamental matter of the nature of the church.

The first principle I adduce which goes beyond this common understanding of the church and gets directly into the heart of the relationship that the convocation has been called to discuss is as follows: Violence is inevitably the child of violence. I repeat: Violence is inevitably and universally the child of violence. Violence is a defiling of human life which is the response of a human being to the defilement of his own life. A murderer feels himself to have been murdered. A thief feels that he has been stolen from. And these violent young men, the Blackstone Rangers, feel that violence has been practiced upon them from birth. The mistake of any nonviolence-oriented organization is to analyze violence as such to be unequivocally and morally repugnant. And any church which too quickly condemns violence has thereby refused to admit that it has, inadvertently perhaps but no less really, been productive of the very violence it condemns.

I find it amazing how city agencies, concerned parents, the police, and a host of individual citizens have risen in a fury of indignation over the violent acts of the Blackstone Rangers. There is a subtle hypocrisy here. The mothers and fathers of the Blackstone Rangers are not considered or condemned for the violence they have practiced on these young men: beatings, hunger, disease, foul and overcrowded living spaces. The violent and despoiling ways of teachers, principals, and counselors of District Fourteen schools have not been considered or condemned, yet they have practiced a daily and deadly role of condemnation on the young men themselves, inspiring a violence they now conveniently deplore. The police are exercised greatly over the lawless hooliganism of the Blackstone Rangers but do not admit their own direct nonsubtle hooliganism, or the role they themselves have played in the development of general ghetto violence. The power structure of the city—by which I mean the administration and its machine, the syndicate, the real estate and commercial interests—this power structure bitterly condemns the Blackstone Rangers without admitting the devastatingly violent role it has played in these young men's lives. The church, this church, has been asked to join with other agencies and the press in condemning the Blackstone Rangers for their violent ways. This church cannot join in the condemnation, for it is guilty of what it condemns. It has stood by mute and watched the procedures of violence develop. No matter how much we now deplore violence, we must preface our repugnance with confession and demand that the accusers of the Blackstone Rangers first join them in the role of defendant, then cast their stones. Violence began with Cain and bears his mark. The moderation of violence is directly tied to forgiveness and not to categorical judgment, is bound to acceptance and not rejection. It seems that we would some day admit in public what we all know so clearly in private. Violence ends when it is no longer produced.

Yet the church has been bitterly denounced for its accepting ways, for having harbored criminals, and so on. The strategy behind such denunciation is clear. The strategy is to practice absolute violence on the Blackstone Rangers toward the vain end of ending violence. Such a strategy produces not nonviolence but riots, burned cities, and a counter violence with an energy all its own. These dread consequences are daily being considered by this church's staff, and toward the end of averting them we have sought to mitigate (with moral and legal power) official strategies which will surely produce them.

The second principle I adduce also goes beyond the widely understood church and its accepted, conventional posture (its sittingness) in the community. This is the principle of identification. First Church has been identified with the Blackstone Rangers. The church has taken their part, has sided with them, has supported them. The identification of the church with the Rangers is true. It has substance and cause. We discovered in the Blackstone Rangers a more-or-less total rejection of the suppressive adult style of ghetto life. We discovered in them a flamboyant rebellion against helping agencies (which destroy), against the hostility of school and police, against employers who assault manhood in exchange for a subminimum wage. We discovered in these poorest of the poor an indestructible ability to envision Woodlawn life in different terms. These poor young men do not believe that life must be and is going to continue to be the way it is right now. As a church we share their belief. Hence our identification. It has followed insight and has required commitment. Not pure commitment in general but ambiguous commitment to a particular ambiguous historical group. I believe this kind of commitment, before the issues are clear, is decisive. It finds its model in marriage, after all, where two young people pledge themselves to a new mutual identity on the flimsiest evidence, not knowing what the other will become, content only to "live it out. . . ." The mutually identified parties change because of the association, as the Blackstone Rangers and First Church have surely changed. We are under obligations, no longer free. The Rangers cannot get us out of their hair. What we are going to say, or do, how we are going to react, are matters the Rangers now have to deal with. The church's consistent denunciation of thoughtless and needless violence cannot be gotten around, for instance. It must be dealt with as a daily substantial fact.. No more can we get the Rangers out of our hair. When we are tempted to be less than morally candid, we have their eyes to look into. When our actions as a church tend toward that vague religiousness, that property conservation and people denunciation for which churches are justly notorious, we have the Rangers there as a harassing reminder of our cowardice. The Rangers will first testify to the immense costliness of the identification. But so can we. Not in the terms of costliness to our reputation or to our property, which are, after all, retrievable and not important, but in terms of costliness to our laissez-faire, status-quo, pass-the-collection-plate-and-say-a-couple-of-prayers style of religious life. The cost to us is that we cannot easily cop out. We are on each other's back. What else is Christian ministry? We shed separating masks in order to share humanity, in order to live in the same space with others, in order to have the same growing up to do toward the model of our poor King Jesus.

The third principle I adduce here is the principle of representation. It is not necessary for a common sense understanding of the church that the church represent itself in peculiar ways to specific constellations of people. It is not even necessary for an understanding of a church-in-mission. We have, however, found representation to be theologically appropriate to the present historical situation. The Rangers represent something definite to us. We represent something definite to them. We present ourselves again or anew. The church is always presenting itself in a general indiscriminate way as something. But when the church presents itself to a specific group, it presents itself anew, directly, i.e., *represents* itself. What are we getting at?

The Blackstone Rangers directly represent Woodlawn as a phenomenally present, discernible reality. The name of the place, in fact, seems to be more like Blackstone Rangers than Woodlawn. That is what the writing on the buildings says. That is what the writing on the minds of Woodlawn residents says, too. These residents are enraged by the Rangers, are fearful of the Rangers. The residents tremble at the sound of the "Mighty, Mighty." But the little children sing "Mighty, Mighty" with enthusiasm. They cannot wait to be Rangers. Residents do not express joy that this is so, but they admit it is so. Let us look more carefully. The Rangers represent the poorest of all: the hungry, the harassed, the politically impotent, the frightened, the badgered, the hopeless. These are precisely the residents of Woodlawn who consistently go unrepresented. The Rangers represent them authentically. No one else can authentically represent them, for no one else displays the reality of Woodlawn.

Obviously, the church in its just sittingness represents *white* power—namely, the whole structure of white American values—and ordinarily fits smoothly within the whole power arrangement, representing a holy legitimation of the American process. But First Church has sought to present anew, to these representatives of Woodlawn reality, the specific reality of the Christian faith. This is a forceful reality. The church has represented the specific hope for the abolition of poverty. The church has presented anew its genuine christological conventions; it has set forth for these particular representatives of the poor the radical messianic vision of humane relations within a humane polis. Within this reciprocal representation the church has had the more radical agenda, radical as the Ranger agenda is. The church has forced the political issue, because of what it represents, upon the Rangers, who are exactly cynical of politics because of what they know it is.

Now let us be clear. Within this reciprocal representation we see very clearly that the traditional agencies in Woodlawn, which claim to represent Woodlawn as a community and its residents, are not representative at all. They represent structures of power located somewhere else. They represent the city, City Hall, the big money, big business, big real estate, the welfare Establishment, and the police. The helping agencies do not help. They hinder. They specifically represent obstacles to what the poor are driving toward, and to the content of the common cause sought by the Blackstone Rangers and First Church. The word "obstacle" has been used here because the helping agencies are usually encountered as passively resisting institutions. Recently we have discovered that helping agencies are capable of aggressive activity as well and have publicly expressed their determination to break up the Blackstone Rangers, the relationship of this organization to First Church, and First Church too, if necessary. In such fashion can we see how unrepresentative, even antirepresentative, these agencies are which sit in majestic counsels, conferring upon one another functions of "representing the poor."

The fourth principle I adduce here is the historically

conditioned necessity for upholding manifestations of corporate ecstatic negritude. This principle flies in the face of what always lay unsurfaced throughout the period when the civil rights movement enjoyed general public good favor: namely, a repugnance for negritude. This repugnance has now surfaced under the banner "back-lash." It now turns out that white people *as* white people do not like Negroes. The way Woodlawn people say it, neither do Negroes like Negroes (pronounced the way WVON announcers pronounce the word: namely, Neee-groes). Black people do not like Negroes. What we are getting at is a time when these Negroes (i.e., colored people who have upward-bounded into the middle class) do not like colored people who have not made it (i.e., black, poor, ghetto people: niggers). No one apparently likes these folks, either Negroes or whites. These black people are the toothache that won't go away. So we are getting at a phenomenon of general public racial hatred, before now seldom disclosed to the naked eye, certainly not encountered (though present) under the mask of lib-erality, tolerance, and gentility experienced at coffee-sip-ping race relations seminars. That mask has been now torn off.

L. D. Jones has said that I have only been a nigger for fifteen minutes and not to get too excited about it. He is accurate, as always. But I cannot follow his advice. Fifteen minutes is long enough. I conceive of this church as one place, and one very important place, perhaps the only place around, where we need not mince words on this subject. We cannot at this time in history stand merely for integrated living or anything like that. All that is the destruction of authentic black people, their living styles, ideas, and aspirations, and the simultaneous creations of white living styles, ideas, and aspirations within black people so that under the banner of integration everybody, black and white, has become white except for the color of the skin, which everybody says is not important anyway. We must, on the contrary, uphold the humanity of black human beings and commit ourselves absolutely to the integrity of this humanity. We see this humanity, uncolored by white diversions and adulterating traits, in the Blackstone Rangers. And uphold it specifically.

One of the Rangers made a penetrating observation on the way back from one of our numerous trips to court. He said: "Polices do not like colored boys." Was he ever right! It is also equally true that schools do not like colored boys. Neither do employers, nor courts, nor white boys. Not even parents like colored boys once they have grown past being cute and can fight. They are feared, misunderstood, and badly underestimated. I say that as a church we must identify with colored boys and young men, exactly as they are, in exactly what they represent, because they are who they are. They enjoy being black. Blackstone is not the name of a street now; it means stone black. They enjoy being together, stone black and young and smart and strong. This is ecstatic corporate negritude. Because of what they are, not in spite of what they are. Let us please not pussyfoot with declarations that we like all boys, and thus the Blackstone Rangers, in spite of the fact that they are black and tend to be destructive. Let us be perfectly frank. We like black boys because they are black.

These are the men of the future. I do not mean by that that they are all going to grow up. I mean they are right now, as youths, the real Negro man, true black men who have not and cannot conceive of a time when they will ever bow down before the white man with a cor-rupting "Yes, massa." These young men have perceived an excellence and hope in the fact of their common black-ness. They do not have to become white or hide a shame that they are black. Somehow they have evaded these traps. They are black, proud of their blackness, and hopeful that they can raise the real issues of being black in white America.

We welcome and encourage such a dramatic power display. The presupposition of reconciliation is the presence of saving truth (delivering truth). God through Christ and the agents of Christ, i.e., bearers of delivering truth, still reconciles the world to himself. Our theological tradition leads us, then, to participate in this reconciling activity going on in our midst. It judges the churches for their general cowardice in not being deliverers and thus functioning as agents of reconciliation. We can in repentance, however, follow at some distance behind where these young men are going.

15

STRANGE

LUKE 24:13–32

The New Testament lection tells a thoroughly Biblical story. Jesus appeared as two of his disconsolate followers were headed home from Jerusalem. He unobtrusively discovered what they were talking and shaking their heads so sadly about. He walked along with them and they didn't recognize him. He was merely a stranger. Now they were talking about their dead—their *crucified*—Master. So the stranger tried to make it all clear to them what had been happening in Jerusalem. He proceeded, in fact, to give them a quick summary of Biblical theology, and I guess you know how that goes, when a stranger whips out one of these vest-pocket Bibles that you need a magnifying glass to read and begins telling you what's in the glorious little book. You are polite but stern and very turned-off. As apparently these two followers of Jesus were when the stranger interpreted scripture for them. They were polite enough. Invited him to stop for a meal, once they reached their destination, and only when Jesus did a characteristic act, entered into a revealing activity, only then did they finally recognize what he was. There is no reason to believe that his voice was different than it had been, or his appearance greatly altered, or that he went to any pains to disguise himself. There is every reason to believe that these two people were unprepared to identify Jesus in the form of this stranger. A thoroughly Biblical story, repeated in varying modes and forms and periods dozens upon dozens of times.

As a kind of intellectual warm-up and to get into the real action of this sermon, I want you to begin thinking about the stranger motif in the western movie. The good man comes into town. He enters the town saloon. There he is greeted with coldness and suspicion. Someone likely as not hits him or shoots at him. Then, inevitably, forces of evil try to use the natural suspicion of the town to focus suspicion on the stranger for a crime they commit. He is then forced to deal with the forces of evil in order to clear his name. In so doing he delivers the town from domination to these forces of evil. The town shows its gratitude by not being suspicious any more, patting the hero on the back. Maidens sigh and things like that. There would be no story at all if the stranger were a bad man. Where would be the surprise? Everyone expects him to be bad, as a matter of course, because that is how strangers are supposed to be. The truly classic versions of this story involve the mask. The Lone Ranger epic. The masked stranger is the object of double suspicion. Silver bullets and white horse do not make the mask any easier to take. There is something about a mask, Robert Frost did not write, that makes you want to tear it off in order to see what secret is being concealed or what mystery lies beneath. Right? Well, do not fear, it never is torn off, and crooks beware. The Lone Ranger is totally 100 per cent good and wins the gratitude of the town. No maidens sigh, because the Lone Ranger is above that sort of thing, and he does after all have his trusted Indian companion. . . .

In towns, in stable communities, the factor of strangeness has been systematically erased. The identity of all the folk is known. The good, the weak, the craven have displayed their true identity, and their neighbors and friends make appropriate allowances or defenses for this identified, expected behavior. People may still perform predictable acts, but they tend to be people prone to that sort of thing, so allowances are made for eccentricity. It is expected. Even communities which have fairly high rates of transiency, with residents staying only a year or so, are relatively stable. Newcomers are evaluated pretty quickly.

In a way, one of the prime tasks of communities is to overcome strangeness, to *domesticate* strangeness, remove its threat and potential danger and provide, thereby, security and dependableness to the residents of the community.

What exactly is the threat? The danger posed by a strange person? He has not announced himself. He has not been identified. You do not know what to expect, therefore. He might rob you, assault you, kill you, or in other fashion do you in before retreating into the obscurity from which he came. He has not been bound in, identified, discussed around the kitchen table or across the bar. He has not disclosed his history, told what he is doing, where he has been, what brought him, what his plans are. So he is unknown. And as long as he is unknown he represents a threat to any prudent group of people..

Now you might think that within the remarkable assimilation patterns of American communities it is easy for a stranger to get known so that he is pretty quickly evaluated as a good person up to no harm, then widely accepted. But you know better and I know better than that. The stranger can remain strange and receive no acceptance even if he lives in nonthreatening ways in a community for ten years or forty. That is, if he persists in his strangeness, if he makes no motions to find out and do what the community expects of him. If he wants to become a member of that community, he is obliged to become like other members of the community. The unacceptable act of strangeness is to make no motions to seek community membership. Communities cannot abide independence, autonomous action and thinking; cannot stand being contradicted; cannot put up with someone who stays in the midst of the community without becoming a member. He is a threat, and a prudent community treats him as the stranger he is, no matter how long he stays or how nonviolently he stays. This is a dimension of the present housing situation that has not received very much attention as so-called open housing legislation is considered in Springfield. It is being demonstrated here and there that Negroes are not dragons, hoods, or garbage scatterers by nature. They can move into communities and rather quickly prove themselves a credit to their communities. Since they cannot really melt into a community and always have the badge of their strangeness in the very pigmentation of their skin, they must work extra hard at being model citizens, deluxe members of the community. What has not been demonstrated is the possibility that Negroes who choose to be independent, remain strange and not participate can *persist* in these basically white communities, without (a) being lynched or (b) going crazy. We see very plainly the premises of communities of men right here. Shape up or ship out. This perdurable conservatism of communities was called tyranny by no less than our co-pastor Harold Walker right here in this pulpit a few weeks ago. So tyranny it is. Whatever, we are nearing the point where we can see some real affinity with the Biblical notion that communities are willful beings, always in need of deliverance. Communities are a natural good that gets corrupted. You look here for the mechanisms which keep sin alive in the human race, not in the biological mechanisms of conception and birth. The natural good and real good of communities is that shelter is provided individuals, a protected place is offered where roots may be put down, nourishment obtained. It is a great thing to be known by all and to know all. It is a good thing to have protectors and tutors, to have a shape into which you are expected to grow. It is a great and good thing to have clearly defined patterns of behavior with equally clear penalties for misbehavior. We are talking about the total shelter provided by a community: the psychological, social, and physical shelter from the tangible dangers of a boisterous world, capable of hatching tornadoes, possessing murderers, felons, social anarchists, freethinkers, and athlete's foot. The good is that human life is protected from tangible danger and, more positively stated, that protected human life will flourish. Joy will abound, peace will be done, and righteousness characterize the dealings of men in their communities. But this good gets corrupted; the community closes off dangers but closes too tightly, so that it closes off the possibility of renewal, strange forms of goodness, and nurture. The good gets corrupted when stability degenerates into regularity and regularity degenerates into ironclad customariness, and ironclad customariness becomes ruthless, forbidding novelty or latitude of interpretation. The emergence of explicit totalitarian societies in our own time and the grim picture of the kind of society we seem to be headed for, e.g., the novels of Anthony Burgess or the well-hailed but slightly heeded *1984* by George Orwell, these totalitarian societies are nothing new under the sun. They are in direct continuity with the communities of men pictured in the Bible, their good corrupted. The security they offer becomes a prison; the nurture they provide poisons initiative; the safety they offer rules out the possibility of significant novelty, difference, conflict, emerging new forms. So the life thus protected turns into something nearer living death. Communities are willful beings, capable of disobedience. Bible communities no less than communities we have known and lived in. And the disobedience is most dramatically evident in the way these communities deal with strangeness, with the stranger. This is why the scene on the road to Emmaus is so dramatic. The risen deliverer, the victorious messiah, strange to Israel only because Israel counted him strange, is not news. He was not recognized in life, in death, now in resurrection. These two people weren't looking for any deliverance in any stranger. They distrusted him; he was intruder, no matter how unobtrusive. His spectacular opening up of the scriptures did not accord with the way they read the Bible. They were grim, obtuse, perfectly representative Israelites who certified themselves as qualified to sit as aldermen on Chicago's City Council, or on the Board of Regents for the University of California, or in any other position of public trust where distrust of innovation becomes a positive certifying virtue. They rejected their deliverer, presented to them in the form of a stranger.

Now, my friends, let us be perfectly clear. God has always presented deliverance to communities of men through the form of a stranger. He does not work from the inside. He does not apparently believe that communities are capable of renewing themselves from the inside out. God puts no stock in the willingness of well-set-up men to make consummate risks. The shriek of dismay we hear not south of the Mason-Dixon line but south of the Canadian border that outsiders are provoking all of this social unrest is exactly accurate. Outsiders *have* provoked the unrest because no one on the inside would do it—if he *saw* it was worthwhile to do, which is equally unthinkable. And God puts as little stock in keeping these chummy totalitarian-reaching communities alive by delivering individuals from bondage. Let us be clear. The only means for deliverance is to break the bondage, and this is not done through the redemption of the individual who somehow can luxuriate magically in a freedom while his fellows stay chained. No. God's dealings with man, God's faithful attempts to deliver him, are all focused on the community as such. The nation, the race, the voting group, the people-as-such. The stranger himself is made eligible by this scripture to be accorded a welcome instead of an automatic denial. Here is what I mean: the strange young we have been producing in such large numbers these days. They do not want to go to college in order to avoid Vietnam *or* in order to get a nice set-up with General Electric. They want once more to have a meaningful choice about going to college, or to Vietnam, or crazy. This is very strange. Not only the dress, the LSD, the music, but the ideas are strange. As though they dropped down on us from another planet, that is how strange they are. They constitute a judgment on us. They accuse us of loving war because war keeps the economy going at a big clip. They accuse us of running propaganda machines and calling them universities. They accuse us of brainwashing. They accuse us of bigotry against races and against individuals. They point out that if most of the great men of past history, including our founding fathers, were alive today they would be harassed or ignored or put on somebody's list. They say our homes are prisons and not havens, that our living areas resemble cemeteries, and they want out. They want to go their own way. And how goes our reaction? Not even polite in our dismissal of their charges. They are not strangers. They are cowards. Rebellious. Traitors. Perverts. Nuts. And that is just the telling reaction the scripture prepares us to look for. Automatic denial. At the very time when it looks like the U.S. will dry up and blow away unless it is seriously renewed.

Let us use the swinging young as the prime illustration

of the ambiguous, strange, potentially delivering sort of people present in our communities. They are the chief example but not the only strange and potentially wonderful people around. Critics, proposers, radical thinkers, radical doers, radical livers—in great assortment: constituting various challenges and judgments on us, banging on the door of our programed minds, urgently seeking admission for an audience with us, somehow caring for us, loving us, and wanting to deliver us from our molasseslike community structures.

I speak directly to the church now and to the arrogance of its pietism. After nineteen centuries of going to church, church people assume that they know . . . where they are going to find Jesus Christ: IN CHURCH, IN THAT BLACK BOOK; and that they are going to know who he is: BLUE EYED, SOLEMN, AND HOLES IN HIS HANDS. Furthermore, they call regularly for the Holy Spirit, either assuming that he is already present or will arrive in such gushy nonmattering ways that the prayerful call is useless or meaningless. There is a monstrous arrogance here. Familiarity. Folksiness with God.

We should be prepared, had we really been going to church and really listening to what is in that black book, for the inevitable divine incognito. We should be prepared for the prophet with dubious credentials. Moses the felon. Joseph in Egypt. A shepherd boy as the king-designate of Israel. The strange Jesus. The strange Paul. We should be prepared, therefore, for the stranger and therefore should search in greater detail, with faithful curiosity, for the stranger in our midst, and listen the more carefully to him when he addresses us—whether he wears a black jacket or a purple bikini.

What good is the Bible and our parading the Bible around, and studying it and honoring it and swearing in Presidents on it, if we don't learn even the most elementary modes of God's activity among men?

166

What good is the resurrection news if we deny the possibilities of its appearance; if, that is, we deny that the resurrection news can assert itself in an actual precinct of the Fifth or Sixth Wards?

What good is our vaunted concern for the poor, for justice, for equality if we deny at the outset the very hidden (strange) possibilities for deliverance? *If* we do not even think deliverance language but think our own program language—thus relying, as Paul would say in his archaic way, on works righteousness?

My first sermon to this congregation was based on a Philippian text which admonished us to strain ahead, to look forward, always examining with joyous scrutiny the contents of the next five seconds, leaning into the future, gripped with expectancy, expecting to be presented then with wonderful eschatological portents—and not the same old thing. Well, it sounded pretty exciting, but it was only a sermon and was fitted thereby into the same old thing as you sat there looking to the past for the cues and clues helpful for evaluating the future. A great existential yawn.

In just such fashion do we ignore the possibilities of faithfulness in favor of our own brand of comfy, non-strange faithfulness. Woe be to us because, when the lightning comes, that won't be mistakable or discussable—unless, somehow, in our symbolic activities, breaking bread, reciting the Our Father, baptizing, we actually do turn 180 degrees away and begin welcoming the stranger. Amen.

16

WORST

In the Old Testament lection we have Jeremiah fetching up his nerve and moral indignation so that he can tell God that he is a miserable God, whose license ought to be taken away. Jeremiah is still a young man, and he still has high idealism about God. Jeremiah believes that God is not only just himself but the guardian of just men, especially just men like Jeremiah, who is a prophet, doing the special work God has called him to do. So what has happened? Jeremiah has been getting pushed around a little. Roughed up. The power structure has begun to react. Jeremiah cannot understand it. All he has done is tell the truth: namely, that all of the priests, soldiers, businessmen, and governmental figures are crooked—you know, nothing but the truth—and what do they do? They get angry at him. Specifically, they try to wangle some land Jeremiah inherited away from him. Call him names. Discredit him. Have Len O'Connor say a few words against him. Start the rumor that Jeremiah is not a real reverend at all, but only a fake reverend. Jeremiah is shocked at this treatment. Almost speechless. This wasn't in the contract at all. So Jeremiah is faced with the same possibilities that David Hume explored. Either God allows all of this

168

evil in the world because he can't do anything about it, in which case he is not very strong, *or* he *won't* do anything about it, in which case he is immoral. Jeremiah has run through these possibilities and decided on the second. God is immoral. He doesn't care. He maybe is on the side of the wicked, anyway. God has allowed one of his prophets to get roughed up, not because he couldn't stop it. Oh, yes, he could stop it. God *wouldn't* stop it. He doesn't care. So Jeremiah has a talk with God. He prays. He really lays it on. "Righteous art thou, O Lord, when I complain to thee." Which, being translated, means, You are the big shot in righteousness, with clean hands and clean heart, but you are only posing. You are putting us on, God. Because "Why does the way of the wicked prosper? Why do all who are treacherous thrive?" Which, being translated, means, Why does the way of the wicked prosper? Why do all who are treacherous thrive? It seems you are on their side. "Thou plantest them, and they take root," says Jeremiah. "Thou art near in their mouth and far from their heart." Which is pretty strong language. Very moral, very thrilling, very satisfying. Jeremiah goes on to suggest that God still has a chance to show his stuff: What can he do to regain his reputation as an honest God who is worth working for? Well, he can slaughter all of those evil people. That's what he can do. Get rid of them. If that were to happen, then folks might have some reason to start believing again.

Great silence. Punctuated only by Jeremiah's breathing. Not only has he made this indictment. He is . . . waiting for an *answer*. So he breathes on for a while, the silence becoming ominous. Then God speaks. "If you have raced with men on foot, and they have wearied you," says God, "how will you compete with horses?" To get the flavor of this answer you must remember how large-scale fighting was done before the advent of gunpowder and airplanes.

Fire and Blackstone

Imagine for a minute some B movies with big fight scenes where huge opposing armies collide. First there are the foot soldiers out in front. They carry spears and big shields. They run all of the time. A lot of them. B movies cannot afford your big-name stars but they can hire a lot of extras at $10 a day, so there are lots of foot soldiers in one army running toward and into the foot soldiers of the other army. And they give a lot of trouble with their spears and there are a lot of them. When . . . whoosh . . . behind them are all of these soldiers on horses, and riding in chariots, with wicked knives on the wheels and big swords hacking away. That is the substance of God's answer to Jeremiah. Here you are having trouble with the foot soldiers, they are giving you a hard time, so how in the world are you going to stand up to the horses when they get here? What is remarkable about this answer is that it is no answer at all. Cheer up, the worst is yet to come. Notice that God is not interested in theology. That whole business about the wicked prospering, he doesn't mention. God is very direct. I called you to be a prophet, not a crybaby. So get busy.

I guess we know already what he is saying. You go to first grade and you think you've really got a lot of stuff to do, drawing all those pictures and learning what one plus one is and following the adventures of Dick and Jane. When you get to third grade and are doing timeses and division and writing regular cursive, and science, you look back on the first grade as a breeze: boy, was it easy, and so on. You get to the seventh grade and you are faced with problems you never dreamed of in the third grade. And the seventh grade will look like a tea party when you make senior year, not only because of all that homework and how much you are expected to know, but also all of the other stuff—which in later years will seem like the best year of your life because it was so easy.

170

You get married and will look back to single living as problemless, and when baby number one comes along, just being married will seem like a Sunday-afternoon picnic. But when baby number three or number four comes along, the time when there was only one baby will seem like only being engaged, and when some of those babies start growing up to become teen-agers, forget any definitions of problems you may have had. They weren't problems at all compared to what teen-agers are. We have some idea of what it means to be wearied by the foot soldiers when a platoon of cavalry is charging in. *Some* idea. But only some idea. The Bible is not saying only: Life gets tougher as you get older. That may be true, but kind of self-evident, and the thing we have to hear. No, we are being presented with something else, something that we may very well not love to hear, that has a lot to do with *being* a church on the South Side of Chicago, at this early date in the time when Negro people are seeking to win for themselves what it is now clear no government will ever give. We do not now live in a time when various groups seek to persuade the government to give money, new housing, consideration, good schools to Negro people— even basic guaranteed constitutional rights. Were we to be living in that kind of time, we could be content with the nonperilous course of gathering weight and then throwing it around. We could get away with welfare programs. Our style could afford to be noncontroversial, even, and vaguely snobbish, delivering our alms of kindness to the poor by way of taxes and Red Feather agencies. But we do not live in that kind of time and have not for a decade. Not all of a sudden has this different time appeared, being announced on television. It has simply begun, and that it has begun becomes clearer all of the time. So we are in this new time when there is a sun-clear realization in the American Negro community that anything worth getting will have to be wrenched away from a reluctant society, *won*. To be a church in this time demands a new style, a new set of priorities, a new vision, and a new stance on the South Side. We have begun to realize this, in the following ways:

1. In the late fifties this church began to see that the welfare style wasn't getting anywhere. That individual churches, or collections of churches, cannot accomplish anything. This church, in concert with other visionaries in Woodlawn, began to see that poverty is not simply a lack of money. It is also a lack of real political power, and this is the poverty that kills. Therefore The Woodlawn Organization was formed as a way to marshal the power of all the people through the agency of collecting the power of all the organizations of people in a large organization of organizations. A stingy and subjugating city in the vision will have to deal with a large and powerful organization and cannot merely pick off malcontents and have its easy way with the community. Thus was created the first large Negro community organization in the world. By any measuring device you want to use, it is still the toughest, most effective, largest, most militant, and promising Negro organization in the U.S.A. That is the new style. The church is not the great white father, throwing its weight around, deigning to give or to withhold, according to whimsey. The church is a participant with other community organizations in determining the course, tactics, and goals of the organization. Reduced from general to P.F.C. This is the new style, and when it happened to Jeremiah, recall, he was outraged and immediately sought an audience with God. Prophets should receive better treatment. So should churches, according to their own members, many of whom want to remain generals. In the South, general is pronounced plantation owner, master, the Man. Up here in the advanced North, general

will do, and many of these folks went off to other churches where the church is the general and a full head and shoulder higher than . . . well . . . Negroes. Well, as the bride said, on learning her husband had cut off his head while shaving on their honeymoon: This is a pretty grim beginning.

2. As the shape of this new time began to become more apparent, the church began to see that there were large and frighteningly powerful youth organizations which were highly provocative, not of mischief but outright streetside violence, and that they were not submitting to the programs that had worked in earlier days. Like basketball—get some uniforms, you guys, and dribble your troubles away—or basket-weaving programs or Aztec-jewelry-making programs or ping-pong. These new youth organizations were not asking for recreation. They were and are demanding their share. Demanding that the whole arrangement be changed. The whole plantation scene wiped out. And this certainly did set up resonances in any justice-admiring churches. But just how does a church go about getting into the large youth organization business? We cannot write Philadelphia to get brochures. Or consult experts, since the experts are still right on top of realities that were contemporary in '58 or '60. How do you do it? You plunge in and try to do the most immediate thing; namely, to reduce the streetside violence and simultaneously clarify the determination of the organization to continue projecting its demands for a change in the system. Well, this demanded a particular style. A relationship as friends. Colleagues, maybe. But certainly not the relation of general to troops, leader to led, master to slaves. And so what happened? Whoosh. All we did was call the existing system evil and hopeless for the mass of Negroes in Chicago: Negro youth, Negro adults, Negro children. Thus all we did was point out the crooked system, and

right away we started getting roughed up. "Why don't you people act like generals?" "Why don't you stick to your business of keeping Negroes in their place?" "What are you trying to do?" And the simple answer is: Change the system, although said in a quaking kind of voice, the least bit shaken, the least bit tired, the least bit worried as we surveyed the damage done to us by various roughing ups or, if you are a purist, roughings up. Right where Jeremiah was. Tired, cross; beginning to be a little doubtful; beginning to think about joining the regular white boss prophets. Well, you see, that is the whole strategy of having the foot soldiers come in first: to produce fatigue, and wounds, and dismay, and a willingness to run away. And then when the horsemen come flying in,, swords whack away, morale and willingness to fight are quickly broken. Jeremiah and First Church, anyone in such a fix, begins to wonder. Their fatigue begins to wonder. Their willingness begins to wonder. Second thoughts. Hurt. Lamenting to God, Why do the crooks always win? and so on.

3. This new time has demanded a style that identifies the church with the aspirations as well as the needs of any justice-serving, justice-admiring segment of the community, and the style of identification is pretty radical. It is not a helping, controlling, masterful, general-type style, so there can never be any doubt about who is helping and who is the helped; the identification blurs the distinction between helped and helper by the very fact of the identification. The distinction, so important to generals, does not amount for much if altogether the church *and* the community *and* its organizations are dedicated to a radical change in the whole system. But what does this mean? That the community begins to identify with the church. Men, women, young people, and children begin to identify the church as their church, the place they go

to, the people they belong to, a whole great big thriving, booming, happy, productive, giving institution. The church gets used. Most churches in the U.S. have a big problem getting people to participate in their programs. This church has a hard time keeping people out. Since November our most critical problem is how to close it down four or five hours out of every day. This is one of the few churches I know about that people break into if you do close it down. But whoever heard of that? A church being used by the community as though it were part theirs. Reciprocal identification. O blessed problems! Breaking into the kitchen, writing on the walls, walking on the floors, O blessed agony! Whoever thought of the price tag? Whoever thought of the problems of many groups meeting and using the church house simultaneously? Whoever can add up in advance the property wear and tear? Like Jeremiah we just plunged right in because this is what the times demanded, and then there is this price tag, these bills, this writing on the walls, this trouble. So is the identification a good idea? Is a multiprogram arrangement a good idea? Would it not be better to go back to the good old days when it was clear which was the church and which was community?

Let us recall last Christmas day. The mighty banquet our ladies served for 500 young men and women on Christmas afternoon, as a concrete expression of their Christmas spirit. It was a wonderful banquet. The tables were beautifully arranged. There was plenty of banquet food. Peace and good will prevailed. But all Christmas week following the banquet the kitchen was subjected to a great deal of extracurricular and unplanned use. These same young men who had been served this fine banquet on Christmas day just kept coming into the kitchen the following days and more or less helping themselves to any of the food they could find. Because they were as hungry on the days following Christmas as they had been on Christmas. And they proved themselves to be terrible housekeepers. Pots were left unwashed. Things were spilled on the floor. Dishes were stacked around. It was a capital mess that the staff came back to after New Year. I cannot judge which was the more prominent: the rage that the kitchen had been used by hungry people who had no business using it or the fatigue which the sight of the mess inspired. It was a nightmare. A little checking around disclosed that there are numbers of boys in this very community who have literally no place to stay in the whole world, no family, no food to eat, no one at all in the whole world caring for them, and *they* had presumed on our unused space and on our unused food. They had messed up our kitchen. Ungrateful? No. They were hungry. Sloppy? Yes. Whenever have they received courses in good manners while a guest? Whenever have they heard about sparkling clean floors and stoves or even elementary lectures on cleanliness? Their experience has been in the other direction, absolutely. The questions began to run the other way. Whenever before have we been concerned for these young men and their non-places to stay and their non-food? Whenever have we bestirred ourselves in the direction of cleanliness for them? The buildings they have lived in, we have allowed to persist in sure deterioration: the rotting hallways, the rotting plumbing, the rotting electrical fixtures. Why should we *now*, all of a sudden, become so vastly concerned at their lack of manners, their apparent sloppiness, their lack of respect for property? Because we are implicated in it, that's why. Because we expected that if they were going to be hungry they would have the decency to take the hunger somewhere else, out of our sight, and express it there, in order that our kitchen-shining sensitivities might not be upset as they surely were on January 2.

So we raised our complaint to God and the Ranger staff, in that order. Why must the price tag be so high? Why have you allowed all of these terrible things to happen to us? And what does God answer? He says by way of subtle clarification that fatigue and disintegration of morale are precisely what the enemy depends on. Make no mistake. The system, the general system, wants nothing better than that we repudiate T.W.O., repudiate the Rangers, repudiate our Excluded Child program. They want us to go back to providing leadership and moral counsel. The system is depending on our tiredness to do us in, our lack of funds, our anger at our sorry fate. This is the gracious word God has intended for our encouragement and strength: Cheer up, the worst is yet to come. Amen.

17

CLIMB

LUKE 19:1–10

I'm giving homework this week. Sorry that I may seem officious about it, but it is time we get this operation tightened up. The book I am assigning for reading and reflection is entitled *Catch-22*, by Joseph Heller, a Dell paper back that goes for ninety-five cents, a book that most of you have read maybe five times already anyway. Any congregation that can't read a book a week because of sitting always in front of the tube has forgotten the meaning of sacrifice and is on the broad way to destruction.

I want you to read this book because I think Joseph Heller is also writing the transcript of the McClellan hearings. I want you to read *Catch-22* because you will find all of his humorous material first in the book, then in the transcript. It is no little thing that a book should be able to touch all the laughter in you, bringing, as it inevitably does, healing and deliverance to you and your house. In fact, it is a great thing that great books seldom do, but that *Catch-22* always will do. That is the nature of salvation. Salvation is what the New Testament is about. That is what this sermon is about. About laughing. So let me give you a taste of the Washington hearings—all prefigured in *Catch-22*. I shall read to you a portion of a trial being conducted against Aviation Cadet Clevinger by a bloated colonel with a big fat mustache.

"One day he [Clevinger] had stumbled while marching to class; the next day he was formally charged with "breaking ranks while in formation, felonious assault, indiscriminate behavior, mopery, high treason, provoking, being a smart guy, listening to classical music, and so on." In short, they threw the book at him, and there he was, standing in dread before the bloated colonel, who roared once more . . . [then] sat down and settled back, calm and cagey suddenly, and ingratiatingly polite.

"What did you mean," he inquired slowly, "when you said we couldn't punish you?"

"When, sir?"

"I'm asking the questions. You're answering them."

"Yes, sir. I—"

"Did you think we brought you here to ask questions and for me to answer them?"

"No, sir. I—"

"What did we bring you here for?"

"To answer questions."

"You're goddam right," roared the colonel. "Now suppose you start answering some before I break your goddam head. Just what the hell did you mean, you bastard, when you said we couldn't punish you?"

"I don't think I ever made that statement, sir."

"Will you speak up, please? I couldn't hear you."

"Yes, sir. I—"

"Will you speak up, please? He couldn't hear you."

"Yes, sir. I—"

"Metcalf."

"Sir?"

"Didn't I tell you to keep your stupid mouth shut?"

"Yes, sir."

"Then keep your stupid mouth shut when I tell you to keep your stupid mouth shut. Do you understand? Will you speak up please? I couldn't hear you." . . .

"Yes, sir. I said that I didn't say that you couldn't punish me."

"Just what the hell are you talking about?"

"I'm answering your question, sir."

"What question?"

"'Just what the hell did you mean, you bastard, when you said we couldn't punish you?'" said the corporal, who could take shorthand, reading from his steno pad.

"All right," said the colonel. "Just what the hell *did* you mean?"

"I didn't say you couldn't punish me, sir."

"When?" asked the colonel.

"When what, sir?"

"Now you're asking me questions again."

"I'm sorry, sir. I'm afraid I don't understand your question."

"When didn't you say we couldn't punish you? Don't you understand my question?"

"No, sir. I don't understand."

"You've just told us that. Now suppose you answer my question."

"But how can I answer it?"

"That's another question you're asking me."

"I'm sorry, sir. But I don't know how to answer it. I never said you couldn't punish me."

"Now you're telling us when you did say it. I'm asking you to tell us when you didn't say it."

Clevinger took a deep breath. "I always didn't say you couldn't punish me, sir."

"That's much better, Mr. Clevinger, even though it is a bare-faced lie. . . ."*

And so on. We are talking about being lost, remember. Clevinger was lost in that court-martial proceeding. He not only was defeated, as were reason and ten centuries of English-American jurisprudence, but his being was obscured, as the being of all the Clevingers is deliberately obscured by what Joseph Heller not-so-humorously pictures as the war system, a regular feature of which is . . . the American

* Catch 22 (*New York: Dell Publishing Co., 1962*), pp. 77–79.

armed forces. Yossarian, Mr. Heller's hero in *Catch-22*, at another place in the novel says that his own commanding officers are his enemies as well as the Germans if his commanding officers send him on suicide bombing missions. The Germans try to kill him. They are his enemies. His commanding officers try to kill him, so they are his just-as-real enemies. Yossarian is lost. Clevinger is lost. They have been designated cannon fodder, their being thus obscured and their desire to live overlooked. You see? Clevinger is Zacchaeus's modern analogue, just as Zacchaeus is for us the prototype of all those people we know who have been unceremoniously bumped from the ranks of the quickly adapting respectable by the quickly adapting respectable, namely the o.k. people. Zacchaeus was in fact considered a traitor. because he worked for the Romans and collected their taxes for them. Kind of Dr. Spock and Jeff Fort in one, you know. Zacchaeus and Clevinger would understand each other immediately. They stand on the same absence of ground outside the community. Thus they know what it is to lose, to be lost, to be without a hope, and certainly without a *prayer*, because they can't pray, leastwise in a church, because church people are in the lead, throwing them out of there and everywhere else.

The story of Zacchaeus, however, does not display a boohooing Zacchaeus, full of self-pity and desire for revenge. He was not actually lost. He was more cast out than lost. His lostness was the result of the way the community felt about him. "He is lost," the people in the community said, meaning, He has no chance of being in *with them*. But he was not lost. He was very much full of juice and had lots of hope. He kept up with the papers and listened to WGRT all of the time. How else would he know that Jesus was coming to town? He heard it on WGRT. Problem: How was he going to see if he decided to go and see

Jesus when he came to town? Zacchaeus was short. People did not like him and so would not let him in the front row, where *they* wanted to stand. Solution: "Get high." Climb a tree, I mean. From there, good position could be gotten on everything. Does that sound like a lost man? To me he seems pretty found. So he was up in this tree, and Jesus did come to Jericho. He shook hands with the mayor, had a brief press conference in which he denied everything, *again*, said hello to the council, all of the great town people, the pillars of Jericho, then saw this Zacchaeus up in the tree. Instantly, he knew the scene. Jesus's whole humanity rose up to the man in the tree. Right past all of the swell people up to Zacchaeus.

"Come on down. I want to stay at your house." A big buzz among the swell people. They, naturally, were disappointed with Jesus. They did not change their minds about Zacchaeus. They knew all about Zacchaeus. Far better than this outside—well, agitator ever could, being in town only minutes. No, they changed their minds about Jesus. What does WGRT know, anyway? And they play such loud music. So rhythmic. Who else was lost that day in Jericho? Jesus. That's who. So these two lost fellows, one just down from the tree, the other about to be nailed to a tree, they walked off toward Zacchaeus's house. Zacchaeus began explaining to Jesus that Jesus was new to the community and ought to know some things before he wrecked his reputation even more. So Zacchaeus started telling him that he was on the House Un-American Activities Committee's list; he belonged to "organizations"; he was not on the best of terms with the local machine; he was the father of a son who had burned his draft card; he had a job which was more socially disapproved than Jesus realized. "You ought to know these things, Jesus, before you come on in. I welcome you. But you should know what you are doing. And you should know that I try to do good. I give half of my goods to the poor, and if I wrong someone, I repay him four times. I want you to know that." Impressive! That was a tremendous exchange of humanity. Jesus acknowledged this with his eyes. No words needed. No nod. His eyes said everything. He walked in.

What if Zacchaeus had been a bounder, a scoundrel who robbed the poor and did wrong without repaying a cent? Would Jesus have just walked in? Well, the story doesn't admit that kind of question. The story says that that is what the swell people do. They make their money off the poor. Their comfortable existence has been secured directly or almost directly by the sweat and blood of the poor. Show me a fortune and I'll show you blood on the money. Every time. The swell people are the ones who institutionalize poverty, who foreclose and evict without thought, who have power and *are* powerful because they have stolen it from the little defenseless people. Ask the question, "Why didn't Jesus stay up on the North Shore?" That's the way to put it. Why did he drift out to some Lawndale or Woodlawn-type apartment on the third floor? The story does not admit the question. The swells are really the really lost, maybe. Maybe they don't like trees. Maybe Jesus couldn't have gotten into the swell houses. The point is, the fact is, here Jesus was, walking into this well-known sinner's house. This super sinner. This Staughton Lynd house. This Jeff Fort house. This Clevinger house. Entering the kingdom of the lost on a vast renewal project. Listen to what he said on entering:

"Today salvation has come to this house."

Feast your ears on those glorious words. They are affirmative, dangerous words, humanizing words, spoken in the domain of the lost. Spoken there alone. Jesus did not say to Jericho before a bank of waiting microphones, "Today salvation has come to your house." The citizens of Jericho would not have been listening. Jesus did not reserve these mighty words for utterance in the temple, for the same reason. There the rich liturgical resonances of these words might have stirred up *avant-garde*-ish goose flesh, but the temple authorities would surely have resented the idea that the temple *needed* renewing or belonged *at all* to the domain of the lost. These great words were spoken where they would be heard, well within the domain of the lost, in the home of a tax collector. Where? At 44th and Princeton; 62nd and Kenwood; 47th Street, anywhere east of Ashland, of course. Where it is at, where humanity teems, erupts, expresses itself in a general lostness because it is existing within a still fully segregated system. These are clearly lost places, full of lost people. Jesus made his announcement to these people in these places (a) because the found, o.k., legitimate folks wouldn't have had him and (b) because they could not receive his words. They didn't want salvation. They still don't. Or understand that they don't want or need salvation. When will Jesus ever get it straight? They want spiritual nourishment and support and quick helps for their mounting ennui.

Anyone, any people, any Christian congregation which professes an adoration for Jesus or has any sense about Jesus being Lord, is going to know where the Christian message belongs and to whom. This was the secret content of the Washington hearings. The Senators, being cued by Chicago police, expressed surprise and outrage that a Christian church would have anything to do with such a lost bunch of criminal scum as the Blackstone Rangers. Well, of course. This was a theological response which Luke nineteen helps us to appreciate. They are pretty swell people, admired, well-known, affluent. They are bound to be offended by First Church, as the citizens of Jericho were offended by Jesus' taking up with that miserable, hopelessly lost Zacchaeus.

Let me start winding up this already long sermon by

reading from another chapter of *Catch-22*. (About the homework: This book has a lot of words in it that are dirty. Not *dirty* dirty words like nigger, love, preacher, self-determination—you know, really vile, profane language. None of these dirty dirty words at all. But it has a lot of clean dirty words in it, most of them four letters long, and I wanted you to know in advance what kind of homework you are getting into.) In this chapter a chaplain to a bomber group in Italy is on the carpet before Colonel Cathcart. And this is what happened:

[Cathcart] "We were speaking about conducting religious services in the briefing room before each mission. Is there any reason why we can't?"

"No, sir," the chaplain mumbled.

"Then we'll begin with this afternoon's mission." The colonel's hostility softened gradually as he applied himself to details. "Now, I want you to give a lot of thought to the kind of prayers we're going to say. I don't want anything heavy or sad. I'd like you to keep it light and snappy, something that will send the boys out feeling pretty good. Do you know what I mean? I don't want any of this Kingdom of God or Valley of Death stuff. That's all too negative. What are you making such a sour face for?"

"I'm sorry, sir," the chaplain stammered. "I happened to be thinking of the Twenty-third Psalm just as you said that."

"How does that one go?"

"That's the one you were just referring to, sir. 'The Lord is my shepherd; I—'"

"*That's* the one I was just referring to. It's out. . . . Haven't you got anything humorous that stays away from waters and valleys and God? I'd like to keep away from the subject of religion altogether if we can."

The chaplain was apologetic. "I'm sorry, sir, but just about all the prayers I know *are* rather somber in tone and make at least some passing reference to God."

"Then let's get some new ones. The men already are doing enough bitching about the missions I send them on without rubbing it in with any sermons about God or death or Paradise. Why can't we take a more positive approach? Why can't we all pray for something good, like a tighter bomb pattern, for example? Couldn't we pray for a tighter bomb pattern?"

"Well, yes, sir, I suppose so," the chaplain answered hesitantly. "You shouldn't even need me if that's all you wanted to do. You could do that yourself."

"I know I could," the colonel responded tartly. "But what do you think you're here for? . . . Your job is to lead us in prayer, and from now on you're going to lead us in a prayer for a tighter bomb pattern before every mission. Is that clear? I think a tighter bomb pattern is something really worth praying for. It will be a feather in all our caps with General Peckem. General Peckem feels it makes a much nicer aerial photograph when the bombs explode close together." . . .

Colonel Cathcart began tramping back and forth reflectively. . . . "I suppose we'll have to keep you waiting outside until the briefing is over, because all that information is classified. We can slip you in while Major Danby is synchronizing the watches. I don't think there's anything secret about the right time. We'll allocate about a minute and a half for you in the schedule. Will a minute and a half be enough?"

"Yes, sir. If it doesn't include the time necessary to excuse the atheists from the room and admit the enlisted men."

Colonel Cathcart stopped in his tracks. "What atheists?" he bellowed defensively, his whole manner changing in a flash to one of virtuous and belligerent denial. "There are no atheists in my outfit! Atheism is against the law, isn't it?"

"No, sir."

"It isn't?" The colonel was surprised. "Then it's un-American, isn't it?"

"I'm not sure, sir," answered the chaplain.

"Well, I am!" the colonel declared. "I'm not going to disrupt our religious services just to accommodate a bunch of lousy atheists. They're getting no special privileges from me. They can stay right where they are and pray with the rest of us. And what's all this about enlisted men? Just how do they get into this act?"

The chaplain felt his face flush. "I'm sorry, sir. I just assumed you would want the enlisted men to be present, since they would be going along on the same mission."

"Well, I don't. They've got a God and a chaplain of their own, haven't they?"

"No, sir."

"What are you talking about? You mean they pray to the same God we do?"

"Yes, sir."

"And He *listens?*"

"I think so, sir."

"Well, I'll be damned. . . . Oh, don't get me wrong, Chaplain. It isn't that I think the enlisted men are dirty, common and inferior. It's that we just don't have enough room. Frankly, though, I'd just as soon the officers and enlisted men didn't fraternize in the briefing room. They see enough of each other during the mission, it seems to me. Some of my very best friends are enlisted men, you understand, but that's about as close as I care to let them come. Honestly now, Chaplain, you wouldn't want your sister to marry an enlisted man, would you?"

"My sister is an enlisted man, sir," the chaplain replied.

The colonel stopped in his tracks again and eyed the chaplain sharply to make certain he was not being ridiculed. "Just what do you mean by that remark, Chaplain? Are you trying to be funny?"

"Oh, no, sir," the chaplain hastened to explain with a look of excruciating discomfort. "She's a master sergeant in the Marines."*

The name of that conversation might be "thugs in the temple." Surely, at a minimum, it displays how much easier, how infinitely easier, it is to proclaim salvation and be heard on 47th Street than in the temple, in church, among religious people, characterized here not by the chaplain but by the colonel. And this is the point I want

* *Pp. 196–200.*

to close on. This giant renewal project announced by Jesus includes the renewal of religion. You just heard a valiant chaplain trying to reclaim prayer for enlisted men, which is to say, for the lost, the sort of people someone might not want their sisters to marry. Niggers. And the chaplain failed. Probably the harder task is standing in religious institutions and saying there, "Today salvation has come to this house."

But I discern it is a task also given to all those who claim Jesus as Lord. And it will remain a task worth doing until all enlisted men, all the lost to whom salvation has been originally proclaimed, begin to humanize religion and transform religious folks *and* their institutions.

Now, if after all this you want to know, practically, What can I do, and what is the concrete issue of this sermon, and what does Zachaeus mean to me; please be specific?—and I'm sure you've seen this coming for fifteen minutes—if you really need my advice on what to do, then my advice is a perfectly scriptural . . . "Go climb a tree!" Amen.

18

BURNED

I Kings 18:17-40

"Do it a third time," Elijah said. Pour on more water. Make it as difficult as possible. Elijah could not believe for a moment that God would provide a small thunderbolt, capable of starting only a tiny fire and that with the driest possible wood. No. "Do it a third time." Would not the strongest supporter of Yahweh suspect that Elijah's behavior might be too much? Say inwardly that such arrogance deserves not to be answered because inwardly he doesn't believe what Elijah believes? These are no doubt the key words in the whole story. We see the whole matter right here. We see Moses going down to Egypt to set Israel free. We see the tribes of Israel fighting the Philistines to a standoff. We see the procession of the exiled Jews returning to the destroyed Jerusalem. And later we see Jesus throwing down the gauntlet before Scribes, Pharisees, Sadducees, and the power of Rome. "Do it a third time." Yes. The key words to this story, and one of the high points in Biblical literature, said by one of the great men in the Bible.

I say that he is arrogant and that his arrogance is refreshing. It proves his greatness. Now just consider how he demolished his opponents, the prophets of Baal. The matchless sarcasm of the words he hurled like stones across the valley, words that the modest and somewhat puritanical translators did not see fit to render into exact English. They were infuriating words because Elijah was insufferable. He was unbelievably sure of himself. He was like—well, I know you are not going to want to hear this—he was like Cassius Clay, who is hardly the most popular man in America today. There are few as unpopular, and the ones who *are* as unpopular are the very ones who are as arrogant as Muhammed Ali, né Cassius Clay. But meanwhile, back to Cassius Clay. And why isn't he popular? He isn't popular in a way that distinguishes him from your ordinary figures. Your Wallaces are understandable, but not Cassius Clay. He defies any theory of explanation. Well, look, Floyd Patterson made their recent fight a religious-type contest. Patterson said he was going to retrieve the championship on the following platform: the honor of the race, the honor of the country, and the honor of the Christian religion. And Cassius Clay agreed to the terms, didn't he? Only he kept calling Patterson the Rabbit and other infuriating things. And then Clay started saying that he didn't want to knock Patterson out; he was going to punish him. Patterson, a dearly popular man with whom the public can identify, kept saying nothing, intent on his training. Came the fight and Cassius Clay did exactly what he said he was going to do and on the terms that Floyd Patterson himself suggested. The honor of the race, the honor of the country, and the honor of the Christian religion were badly tarnished because Patterson lost. Not only lost, he got whipped, threshed, clobbered. If you need a modern parallel in order to understand this Biblical story, then this is the one to consider: it is Cassius Clay who says "Do it a third time," go ahead, drown that wood with water. I'm going to win. I'm the greatest.

And that kind of understanding puts the opening of the story in a somewhat different light. Remember, the king

Ahab meets Elijah and says, "Is it you, you troubler of Israel?" Now just pay attention to what Ahab is saying and do not rush ahead as Felix Mendelssohn did and throw in enough lush chords and trombones and kettledrums to drown out critical thought. Ahab spoke for himself, he spoke for his wife Jezebel, and he spoke for the people who had developed a real fondness for the weird new gods that Jezebel had brought with her from her native land. He represented, as it were, the Roman Catholic Church, the National Council of Churches, the American Association of Evangelicals, the U.P.I., the A.P., the whole United States Government, the American Legion, the N.A.M., all the labor unions except the teamsters and electrical workers and longshoremen, the Democratic Party, the Republican Party, the Boy Scouts of America, the Association of Tavern Owners, and the Morticians of the U.S.; pretty much everybody. You see, troubler of Israel meant *established* Israel, Israel officialdom, as much or more than it meant, merely, the king. When we read this story we tend to identify with Elijah and his cause. He is, after all, the hero. But I am pointing out that this is not being fair. To get the right feel of the story we should be identifying with Ahab and his good politics of pluralism; every religion is all right, live and let live. Elijah, I suspect, would be labeled an unseemly troublemaker by our own United Presbyterian Church. We would nod our head vigorously with Ahab when he said "you troubler of Israel."

But does such a concentration of power as Ahab represented ruffle Elijah? Well, what if Lyndon Johnson were to ask Cassius Clay to keep his big mouth shut, just what do you suppose Cassius Clay would answer? He would answer, I dare say, with pretty high-spirited irreverance, like Elijah, "Up yours, Lyndon." Elijah, with that provocative assurance of his answers, "*I* have not troubled Israel; but you have, and your father's house, because you have forsaken the commandments of Yahweh and followed the Baals." I keep bringing in Cassius Clay because he helps us appreciate the Biblical material. Also he helps us understand the parallel. Cassius Clay is not an Elijah figure. Repeat: *not* an Elijah figure. He is like Elijah in one important respect: namely, he has chosen to go against the national grain. He has challenged the whole establishment and infuriates everybody but the members of his personal entourage, numbering in the hundreds, some Muslims here and there, and a good many poor people he keeps helping. Everybody else dislikes him with a passion.

So, leaving the modern world behind, let us plunge onward into this great story and what it portends for us. The writer of the story did not find Elijah arrogant or even self-assured. The writer was sympathetic to Elijah's program of upsetting the king and his idolatrous wife. The writer, too, believed in the absolute sovereignty of the Sinai Covenant, just as Elijah did, so the writer pictures Elijah as the inevitable winner. From the writer's point of view, it is nothing that Elijah says, "Do it a third time." Elijah could have set that fire with weighted rocks and firewood in a snorkel outfit fifty feet under water in the Mediterranean Sea, and it would have made no difference. The fire would have been started. The prophets of the Baals would have lost because the writer knows with the certitude of all Hebrew writers that the Baals are phony gods who cannot deliver in the clutch. Your Baal god will blow it every time. It is not Elijah's self-assurance—verging on arrogance— which is the point of the story, anyway. *We* find it fascinating, but not the Bible. The fascinating thing as far as the Bible is concerned we do not find fascinating at all, but maybe boring and certainly impertinent. Here is the main part of the story as far as the Bible is concerned: Elijah's speech to the people who gathered at Carmel for the contest.

Said Elijah, "How long will you go limping with two different opinions? If Yahweh is God, follow him; but if Baal, then follow him."

The people said nothing. Like us they are bored when the serious part comes. So Elijah said, All right. You will not make a decision. You do not think that a decision is necessary. You have already decided for Baal. You will not be serious about anything and want only spectacles and must have your spectacles in living color, so I, I alone, "am left a prophet of Yahweh; but Baal's prophets are four hundred and fifty." Let us have a contest.

The question was: How long will you go limping with two different opinions? The most charitable way to put it, because Elijah alone in all Israel kept one of those opinions alive. The Covenant narrowed down to one man, one representative man, confronting the enemies of Yahweh in solitary might. The Covenant demands for peace and righteousness concentrated in this one man, his speech and his action. But still *one* man and a no one at all and still one rather spectacular man. Now what is perhaps offensive about this is that Israel was only limping along on two opinions because it was against its will being represented by Elijah. Someone was taking the Israelites' place, acting in their behalf. So then they were cast in the role of spectators in the balcony, only watching the mighty events as they unrolled. They acted in behalf of the observers. We can see how this goes. During the early days of the civil rights struggle, individual clergymen would join, participate in demonstrations, and end up in jail. They were on occasion ministers of congregations, and they got their names in the papers as ministers of those congregations. In the eyes of the public communications media, they represented the position of their congregations, and they did. But oh, the hue and cry of the congregations! "No, sir. He doesn't represent me! Just because he got this hare-brained notion and arranged to get thrown in jail and all of the papers pick it up does not mean that he represents me." We see how it goes. There is a point at which people resent being represented, especially when their representative is doing and saying things antagonistic to their own cherished beliefs. But on a deeper level their representatives are acting because of the demands of our Covenant faith. In the time of Elijah, because the king had instituted bureaucratic policies antagonistic to public practice and oppressive to the people. Because, some pious Biblical writers said, he allowed the foreign gods into Israel. But really because he became himself insensitive and inhumane, so that the public peace and the righteousness of the nation were distorted by his autocratic will.

Although the people who gathered around to hear Elijah's great speech were in no condition to understand his good news and in no mood to rejoice, their own best interests and the future of Israel were being well served by this one still-faithful representative man.

And although the people gathered around to hear Jesus' great speeches were in no condition to understand his good news about the sovereign loving power of God, and in no mood to rejoice, their own interests, too, and the future of Israel were being well served by this one still-faithful man.

In the name of revolution by prophets, Elijah challenged the people to return to the foundations of Covenantal life. And some, when Jesus was in Palestine, wondered if Elijah had not returned to earth because he laid out the issue in just this way and made the issue of what God was doing—hence, *his* kingship, *his* soverign will, the crystal clear and single issue of all human life, individual and corporate.

As Elijah had challenged the monarch, so Jesus by the arrogance of being born forced the mighty Herod into such rage that he slaughtered the innocents in order to cast a net big enough to catch his infant rival. And, as Elijah, so Jesus won a mighty victory. Not for the TV cameras. How can you say "Do it a third time" so that TV can understand that? How can you say Immanuel so that TV could possibly understand? How can the whole Christmas event be understood by the merchants along 63rd Street with their fantastically non-Christmas, pseudo-Christmas, one-eighth Christmas, anti-Christmas music? I think we'll have to grow earlids to keep it out, really. The point being the strange victory, in fact, the action of God, is not picturable, or tape-recordable. It occurs in the private parts of and only in the silent reaches of men's hearts, where men decide and decide again and decide again that God is King.

You know how it turned out. The firewood burned. Yahweh prevailed, and in prevailing made opportunity for belief possible once more for those who stood by, and for us, too, as we ponder the strange victories of a mighty God. Amen.

19

PEACE

My friends and colleagues around the country have really had their eyes scorched this week. They are worried and angry! To think that that old Senator is messing over their friend John Fry, old pure-hearted noble John. Well, to all of them I say thanks for the concern. But they sure are late. And ignorant. I mean my white friends are ignorant. They think the rules of the committee are "unfair." That the Senators conducting the investigation are unkind to a clergyman. Why, they actually called him preacher, as though that were some term of reproach. Well, every one of you who got burned up this week also got taken in. You really think the issue is my character, my motives. And most of you believe that I am innocent of these fantastic charges. Good for you. I really am. But you have also been taken

---

This sermon was delivered on June 30, 1968, the first Sunday after I returned from testifying before the Senate investigating subcommittee chaired by Senator McClellan. The subcommittee was supposedly "investigating" an O.E.O.-funded youth project run by The Woodlawn Organization. The First Presbyterian Church, however, appeared to be the primary target throughout the first few weeks of the hearing.

in, because you think that is the issue. Ignorant, gullible, good-hearted people. You think the U.S. is still run by rules and that nice people triumph in the end. You think that a whole flock of telegrams to Senators will impress them to do something, just like you learned in high school social studies. Well, grow up.

What you saw and read this week is not unusual or surprising. Go on down to the boys' courts and the criminal courts of Chicago or any big city and you will see what Chuck and Ann and I have been seeing for two years. We have been seeing black people, good people but black people, standing up there all alone, charged with crimes. We have been seeing slick investigators drone through their smooth testimony, and it is taken like it has got to be true because the investigators have—well, a badge on their shirts or tucked in their wallets. But the black cat on the stand, he can't say two words till he is jumped all over and ridiculed and torn apart by these blue-eyed prosecutors as though because he has been charged with a crime and he is black—well, he has got to be guilty. Every day it goes on. Fancy commissions investigate all of this stuff and put out fancy reports, but it still goes on every bloody day. What I went through, what Chuck went through, is *nothing* compared to what many of our black friends have gone through, lots of times. So grow up. I mean they have gone through it without national publicity, which wouldn't help any because they don't have big-shot friends. I mean they have gone through it and lost. I tremble to think how many perfectly innocent people are convicted and serving sentences right now. They are criminals when their only crime was being black. I tremble to think not only of them but of all you outraged people who weren't outraged early enough.

This church has been made to appear an evil place, or chamber of horrors, because we have gone banging right down to those very courts and tried to provide minimal constitutional protections to black young American citizens charged with crimes. And not just any black young American citizens but Blackstone Rangers. Wow! Double, triple, terrible crime. I mean the computer fuses just blow out when you put church and Blackstone Rangers in the same sentence. Why? Because the business of the church is not to mess around with anything important, like saving lives or justice, or a better life. No, sir. As Lieutenant Edward Buckney confessed in a *Presbyterian Life* article. Well, let me read a bit of that article:

If First Church is doing the wrong thing, then how can concerned churches work with gangs? They can't.

How can other social agencies and groups work with gangs? They can't.

Then who can work with gangs? The police.

How can churches and other groups help the police work with gangs? They can't.

Of the many different efforts now being made in Chicago to deal with gangs, which have been the most helpful to the police? The formation of the Gang Intelligence Unit.

What can be done about gangs? They must be broken up.

If a church should find itself with a gang on its doorstep, what should it do? Call the police.

What should First Church do for the youth of Woodlawn? Organize a youth fellowship.

What should it do about the Rangers? Nothing.

Who will do something about them? The police.

What will they do? Break them up.

There it is, partly exposed. But not all exposed. No. Not yet. You know who stands to lose most? Just think about it: who stands to lose most if the Blackstone Rangers and East Side Disciples are strong and at peace, not only talking about black power but doing black power, and turning their communities around, and getting the brothers together and away from each other's throats? You know who. No killings, no shootings. No black statistics. Who would be directing traffic again? The officers now involved in maligning the Rangers.

Let's let it all hang out while we are at it. They don't figure this church out. They cannot believe that we love people. I mean *love*. Care for. Work, sweat, die for people because we love them. We are here to love people. This is not hard to understand, is it? A church is people under divine command to love. Did Jesus Christ come as a king, a senator, a general? No. A servant of all. And that is what the expert on urban affairs, Senator Mundt, called a chamber of horrors. Dig? Love is horrible. And black love is well . . . dirty. They think the business of the church is to go to lunch with the Mayor and give opening prayers to the American Association of Manufacturers. They do not even think of the poor in jail, without food, evicted, in need of hospitals that won't accept them because they need help but are broke and black. They don't understand the church and want the church to retire to the pastures of safe, pious irrelevance. So grow up. The Senate of the U.S. may not like our church, but that is not the issue. Do they like black folks? Woodlawn? Ghettoes, cities, or poor people at all? Certainly the subcommittee has shown little enthusiasm for *that* issue. They don't want us to love each other and protect each other. They don't want us to work together. The poor things need loving themselves, and I wish they would come over here and share with us the problems and promise of our common life. So grow up and find out what our Lord was talking about. The most dangerous thing you can do is love. The world isn't ready for it. Greed it can manage. Lust it can understand. Hate it thrives on. Meanness makes it go around. But the world is enraged by love. So grow up and watch out.

And you better believe they do not understand peace, how we honor peace and truth and black dignity. Well, look, we did everything we could, I mean *everything*, for peace in Woodlawn. We even let law enforcement people use our wall safe in order to get some weapons out of circulation. In the interest of peace. What else? We only had valuable papers in there. What better place than a church whose Lord is the prince of peace? Well, you know the world isn't very much ready for peace. So we are getting still knocked around for that disarmament because the church maybe should be for war. Maybe we should just have let the thing go. Not bothered. Not exercised ourselves in behalf of peace. Not tried to establish a climate in which peace can flourish. But there we were in this love for peace, and there were the authorities who have the responsibility for maintaining the peace very upset at us. To this very day. They see black people killing black people all the time, and that does not seem to bother them. Shoot to kill. Or, toned down: *Mostly* shoot *mostly* to kill. Right? That's O.K. But try to get some peace, and bam! There you are, being insulted and torn apart in the press. Peace in the black community is not comprehensible. I told Senator Mundt about how Thunder Stevens last September maybe saved a lot of lives and millions of Chicago property dollars, and the Senator was hardly listening. He wanted to get to Thunder's criminal record. Dig? Jeff Fort staved off a race riot, and Gang Intelligence Unit right away figures he did it to extort merchants. "Opportunity, Please Knock" played right here to pleased, cheering audiences, and the police say they did it to buy submachine guns. Everything that the Rangers have ever done to make this life better has been twisted by official interpretation to come out bad and warlike. Most of the little fighting that has been going on for the past months has been instigated by detective-inspired rumors. Guys who need to see bleeding black flesh, I guess. Who don't yearn for peace, work and pray and put their own lives on the line for peace. So grow up, you peaceful and peace-striving Christian people. You invite the wrath and power of your elected representatives when you work for peace. They haven't the sophistication to understand such simple motives.

Now I want to make a confession to you, the confidentiality of which is somewhat marred, but nonetheless a confession. Especially you who know me best know my rather large capacity for instant anger and flamboyant language when enraged. And thus were surprised that I just kind of sat there this week. It wasn't because I wasn't mad. I really was. But you see this church belongs to a very powerful organization known as The Woodlawn Organization. We are only one of 120 member organizations in that great Woodlawn Organization. The president of that organization is no honky preacher, who fiddles with his glasses and otherwise waits. No. A honky preacher belongs to the organization and fiddles with his glasses, because I knew what probably few others outside Woodlawn know: that the president of T.W.O. is going to be up there in that chair. And he is just about the finest black man and the maddest black man in this country. Julian Levi two Saturdays ago called the Reverend Brazier one of the five top citizens in Chicago. I'll up that. Reverend Brazier is one of the five top citizens in the country. He's going to Washington tomorrow. And the glory of the Lord will be all around him, and the heavens will crack in two if the truth is not heard. So grow up. Jesus Christ chooses to speak through a black man, and Jesus Christ told me to keep my white mouth cool. Blessed be the name of Jesus Christ forever. Amen.

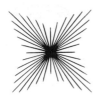

PART FIVE

Judgment in
Our Times

20

JUDGMENT IN OUR TIMES

As the United Presbyterian Church starts getting itself together for one more great General Assembly, I notice this one thing: That the urban-racial crisis has got a lot of glamour. By glamour I mean appeal, interest, excitement. Riot-watching and riot-expecting are fascinating activities. Violence-hungry Americans—violence-hungry *Presbyterians*—really go for riots, while of course expressing ostentatious revulsion (in much the same way that they are horrified by the use of napalm but secretly dig it). You know what I mean? Had no reaction to Martin Luther King flamed up all over the newspapers and television of the land, why, we might possibly have felt let down. And wondered whether we have a serious crop of Negroes or not. In fact, the revulsion over property damage and bloodshed which *apparently* coursed through all flag-loving folk as Washington, Chicago, Memphis, and, belatedly, Kansas City started

---

This address was delivered at the Pre-Assembly Conference on Evangelism when the General Assembly of the United Presbyterian Church, U.S.A., met in Minneapolis in May, 1968.

burning, this revulsion was pretty lip-smacking. Let me get right at it. I think decent, very white, and super Presbyterian America *lusts* for a long hot summer. A very long, very hot summer. For the same basic reason this America positively loves professional football and war.

I hope this way of beginning does not put you off. I do not intend it to. I want to call into public consciousness these preliminary matters. The urban-racial crisis is fascinating. The prospect of fire bombs, Molotov cocktails, sniper fire, Mace, the whine of sirens, the 72-point-type headline is exciting. Gutsy kids, dangerous and furious black men, furious and dangerous police, television cameras smashed, cars being tipped over, white people assaulted, killed, have appeal, zap-power. Whole blocks in flames, more sirens, Federal troops charging in, National Guard units mobilized, guerrilla warfare, statements by mayors, statements by governors, statements by the President, so dense with automatic rhetoric, are—well, glamorous. Because we have successfully turned the urban-racial crisis into a spectacle, we have a new frontier (not a political crack) with real people using real bullets—not like *Gunsmoke,* where they fire blanks and use catsup for blood— a new frontier *and* a circus with trapeze artist (fireman) and dancing bears (looters). Which is quite a trick: to transform a terrible agony into entertainment. But then this is a tricky country. As was Rome.

For the church this urban-racial crisis has additional glamour because the church can elbow its way into a piece of the national spotlight again with its crash programs and task forces, with its hot and cold running ministries guaranteed to be relevant by *Good Housekeeping* magazine. Glamour and cash. They go so well together, and explain each other, precisely like gin and vermouth, police and brutality, Negro and dancing. Glamour and cash. These new ministries are going to be costly, commissioners. Be prepared for that. Poor people's marches cannot be surveyed and managed on peanuts, you know. The urban-racial crisis means something almost like a racket: the glamorous come-on, then the hit.

And what do we have asserted here in these preliminary remarks? The total estrangement between white and black America. That is number one. And, number two, the United Presbyterian Church's unalterable position safely within the precincts of the white side. Let me show you what I mean, by recalling the church's role in the Chicago riots on the weekend following Martin Luther King's murder. 1. The church sought to establish rescue stations for homeless, distraught, and burned-out residents of the West Side. 2. The church appealed to its members and friends to give food, clothing, bedding, and money—which they did in abundance. 3. The church in a few instances was a target of black wrath, and as an ironic consequence some high-ranking clergy will be having to testify against the very finest black men on the West Side, accused as they are of arson. 4. The church expressed corporate guilt from its pulpits and belatedly began to hail Martin Luther King. 5. The church in a few instances kept the peace, or at least tried to. 6. There is no six. There is no record of the church having participated in the violence. No six at all. No Presbyterian ministers or laymen were arrested for arson or looting, because none of them did any arson or looting. This was convulsive controversy, I remind you. Portentous. Bespeaking terrors to come. Wild destructions, conflagrations. The merest beginning of general civil agony. The moon is often afraid to come up in Chicago. The most serious series of events in Chicago's history, including its last fire in 1871. And the church? As Chicago absolutely polarized into black and white communities, where was the church? The church was on the side of the city, on the side of civilization, on the side of property, on the side of law and order, which is the side Dr. King's murderer apparently is on, too, *against* the furious black people on the

West Side. There! The church put itself irrevocably on record. It lost any footing it ever had in the black community. It copped out when the heat was on.

We see demonstrated here the white America that *watches* riots from *afar*, transmuting them into entertainment, with the church very much in the center of white America, and for that simple inescapable reason against black America. So here in the church I conceive all of this concern about the urban-racial crisis as a brilliant fake.

When push comes to shove, we have been, are, and probably will continue to be pastor to white America, which in structure, style, and content is racist, much more profoundly and thoroughly than the Kerner Commission ever dreamed or let on. Nowhere do I find a more revealing portrait of racism than the assumptions with which United Presbyterians come to this General Assembly. These assumptions are that the church is on the side of the *answer* to the crisis; that the church is on the side of the resources and power; that the church gives its resources, its answers, its programs, its power to the *problems:* namely to the resourceless and the powerless. The fact that you have invited great and good black men to address you does not alter these racist assumptions. These men appear as co-opted resources and will be too gentlemanly to tell you anything.

We do not *have* to go into the obvious matters, I suppose, in order to discover where and how we stand. But we must.

There was an altercation in Chicago last fall between citizens which two police officers sought to break up. In the scuffle there was gunfire. One of the officers was wounded slightly. The two of them began chasing a man they thought had used the gun, chased him through alleys and buildings right into his own apartment. He had hidden himself in his apartment. In a very shallow closet. So shallow that he had to elevate his arms over his head for the door to close. The police officer searched the apartment. Came finally to the closet. Opened the door. "Halt," he said, to the man standing before him with hands empty and already up. "Halt," he said and fired four shots into the black man at point-blank range and finally fired two gratuitous shots into him, already dead as he lay on the floor. The officer was in hot pursuit of a dangerous man, the man they *think* wounded a policeman, which makes lethal retaliation O.K. but adds no solace to the mourning family.

I bring another report of the fantastic and illegal lengths the city of Chicago has gone to for the purpose of beating down organized black resistance. The Blackstone Rangers, four thousand strong, represent creativity and hope for every black poor person in the city. And yet they are beaten, illegally jailed, given high bonds, crucified in the press—yes, and killed in a vain effort to break them up. The whole legal, political, and social system enthusiastically supports the effort. While people of good will avert their eyes and get cheerlessly drunk every night.

From the vantage point that white America occupies, so far away that no shots are heard, this report is greeted— how? With indifference born of the knowledge that nothing can be done. But indifference, nonetheless. On a side, nonetheless. The side of a system that day by day elaborates its evil projects in our presence if not our knowledge. We have succeeded in keeping our precious distance from day-by-day brutalities. As a consequence, we allow a free hand to those who are immune to the interests of law and order so carefully preserved in other, more pleasant communities. We have succeeded in keeping ourselves unsullied, because others dirty themselves in our place. We hire thugs, and, balancing the accounts, we too are thugs, the worse thugs for our distance and indifference. Without us, such men could never carry out deeds that damn us as much as they shame these men.

Please multiply the horrors which befall black people

who live sequestered in *our* cities. Use a calculus humane enough to comprehend that it is horror which is being multiplied; multiply, however, these horrors into their true enormity—these brutalities, indignities, sadisms; these rapes, thieveries practiced upon black people—until they fill the earth. And then we shall the better see that we are not only safely within the precincts of white America, its pastor, but *also* that this is an armed camp we are in, full of guns and clubs and Mace. Yes, the lovely suburbs, beauteous homes, casual and what we call gracious living: this is an armed camp. We have the capability to conduct violent assault on black America. We have the capability, if not the stomach, to conduct genocide. That is our side, the side of white America.

So, you see, what was revealed in the Chicago riots is more ominous morally than we perhaps realize. The church was not identified at all with the black poor and their momentary incendiarism but with white power and its regular—matter of course—incendiarism, which it calls law and order. The urban-racial crisis has been created by this law and order. By Chicago's Mayor Daley and all his counterparts. And by all who elect him and keep him in power. By the churches which participate in his system. Many a policeman in this country could well wear a button right next to his star on which would be written: "Compliments of the Christian church. Jesus Saves."

Just how then do *we* propose to address ourselves to this crisis? How can *we* picture ourselves in the role of power, resources, answers when we are the ones who have produced the crisis? Will not our efforts inevitably express white power no matter how generous? Can we somehow evade the consequences of our sinister role by way of pronouncement? Let me quote at length from Karl Jaspers, a German philosopher who wrote *The Question of German Guilt* after World War II and obviously had other, impending, genocides on his mind as he pondered the total guilt of Germany and all Germans in killing six million Jews. He wrote:

There exists among men, because they are men, a solidarity through which each shares responsibility for every injustice and every wrong committed in the world, and especially for crimes that are committed in his presence or of which he cannot be ignorant. If I do not do whatever I can to prevent them, I am an accomplice in them. If I have not risked my life in order to prevent the murder of other men, if I have stood silent, I feel guilty in a sense that cannot in any adequate fashion be understood juridically or politically or morally. . . . That I am alive after such things have been done weighs on me as a guilt that cannot be expiated.

Somewhere in the heart of human relations an absolute command imposes itself: In case of criminal attack or of living conditions that threaten physical being, accept life only for all together, otherwise not at all.

No theological daintiness, which we might recognize in the garb of gradualism, can survive the rigors of this kind of analysis. At this late date we cannot interpose the multitude of our good works between ourselves and the reality of this guilt. Not our pronouncements, our programs, our ministries, our money. Not anything. We are mutually, equally, homogeneously, and simultaneously participants in a system of evil which has now come to a critical point. We are mutually, equally, homogeneously, and simultaneously guilty of monstrous crimes; I mean murders, beatings, rape, exploitations, savagery, incalculable brutalities. Guilt is the leading thematic characteristic of our being where we are and who we are in contemporary America. It makes no difference that we acknowledge the guilt. It is objective fact, ready to be found, accepted, or dismissed, but there as a substantive presence. So what are we doing here with our vain and condescending concern for the urban-racial crisis? Expressing a denomination-wide guilt.

In such fashion do we come to the subject of this talk,

which is Judgment in Our Times. We come on the side of guilt. Not as theological spectators, or moral experts, which we manifestly are not. Judgment does not just occur, you know, producing guilt. The guilt comes first and is the occasion for judgment. We are guilty ones who face now a judgment for our participation in the ugliest imaginable crimes. Nor do we come before God and his judgment. We cannot face God. Nor can he face us, so deep is the alienation between us. Yes, that would be Armageddon. And we do not come before divine surrogates, either, ritualistically confessing sins between yawns and automatically accepting a forgiveness we neither believe in nor care for. Our guilt commands us to the prisoner's dock. Or else we are not serious about judgment in our times. In the seat of judgment sit the colored people of this land; not some reverend old fuddy-duddy but hot-eyed black people. I mean Rap Brown, the Blackstone Rangers, mothers of slain sons, wives of slain husbands, Stokely Carmichael. We would prefer a different situation, no doubt. Were we not guilty it is possible we could demand better accommodations. All of the gestures of a 300-year-long fantasy of white superiority incline us to want to get up into the judgment seat and tell *them*, the blacks, what the judgment is. "You get yourselves educated; get some sense of time so you get to work on time. Clean up, shape up, forget watermelon, and stop having so many kids!" But in this present action we are the guilty ones, and our judges are the primordial victims. The living and the dead. I have it on good authority that the Tuskegee Institute has conducted an elaborate historical search and has determined that 50,000 black people have, since Reconstruction began in the South, been violently killed, principally by lynching; they were not tried because they were not accused; they were not accused because they had done nothing. That they were . . . that they were black was sufficient. Yes, those 50,000 rise up and stand with the living to search us. It has been established. We are guilty, all right. But now they search us to determine why we have allowed these monstrosities to persist. *Why* were we silent? Why were we busy? Every nigger joke comes back now to perplex those who judge us. What reason can we give for condemning black Presbyterian pastors to penury, to servitude? How could have stood by? Yes, and the apparently innocent who have removed themselves farthest from ghettoes, the suburbanites and exurbanites, how could they have valued their peace so highly while thousands of black children in Mississippi live below marginal starvation levels *tonight?*

Obviously we will not improve our case by asking in such deceptive innocence, "What can we do to help you?" Our judges *know* that we have no intention of helping. I guess this earnest question, "What can we do to help you?" is the most enraging event of all. For the people who ask this question will give little and take much. I will tell you of churches filled with affluent, powerful people, who might have made enormous contributions to the cause of racial justice in this country but did not. They continued to go into cities and rifle them of their wealth, continued to work with corporate and political structures which are actually pirates and vultures: bitterly and cynically racist. These men and women would do nothing about that, so that all they might have done is give money and instead of giving it have invited some exciting inner-city types out to address their various groups and paid $25. Do not dare ask "What can we do to help you?" For the tables have been turned and it is the Christian church and the white America it has so resourcefully served which must await a verdict and hope against hope for mercy.

Now of course we need not face this judgment. We have the guns, you know. We can treat the whole matter of racial guilt as a theological opinion and walk away. This was Israel's response to guilt. It is, in fact, a human and almost universal response to guilt: to despise it, question it, repress it, whether the guilt be real or neurotic. But see, until we do actually and freely enter the dock and publicly acknowledge guilt, there can be no judgment. And without judgment there can be no acts filled with repentance, no cleansing of our foul hearts; consequently there can be only Armageddon. It is, I know, a peculiarity of religious people to *long* for Armageddon, which they mistakenly call peace and the end of woe. At bottom such a longing to have done with problems is merest evasion, the existential motions of people trying to escape the twisting coils of guilt. "The Fire" may indeed come "next time"; if it does it will have been brought on by the moral cowardice of white and Christian America, both unwilling and unable to make public acknowledgment of its guilt.

What might the judgment be? How many of us shot for our villanies on the spot? How many of us stripped of our positions? How many elegant housewives forced to clean their maids' floors and toilets? How many tycoons sentenced to jail for 299 years, there to ponder their cruelties? How many church buildings burned to the ground, their ashes salted, because they rejected so much as one black Christian by overt or covert deed? How many billions of dollars in reparations? We do not know. We are not the judges. We are the guilty.

Let us however, I beg, submit to such judgment in order that justice be fully done, the justice of each black person fully satisfied. And having endured the agonies of true penance, having been cleansed of our guilt, then join hands and seek as brothers to do our father's will. The last shall be first; the downtrodden seated at the head of the table; the wounds of the afflicted healed; the sorrowing comforted; the hungry fed. Will the church take this step? Will the church come to enjoy the sound of black and white together, the prospect of neighbors loving each other, the thought that the poor and hearty Lord Jesus will once more be confessed in his church? But until we have been judged and paid the full price, we shall continue to persevere in our reckless white arrogance and court the sure destruction which history stores up against tyrants, even tyrant churches.

21

SIGHT

This story you have just heard has duplicates in all three synoptic Gospels. Christian writers seemed to revel in the cure of blindness, inasmuch as it was such dramatic and clear evidence that Jesus is the Christ. The merely medical aspects of the healings are of no great concern to this or any other New Testament writer. They are—all of them—greatly concerned to show that Jesus *as the Christ* inaugurated the new time of God in which it had been promised the lame would walk, the prisoners would be visited, the hungry would be fed, the poor would have the good news preached to them, *and* the blind would receive their sight. These writers were not subtle. They sought to depict the event so that it would have moral-universal consequences. They were saying that spiritual blindness is involved. The enemies of Jesus thus appear in these stories as the most blind because they cannot even "see" that a blind person received his sight at the merciful hand of Jesus. And Jesus is presented as being powerless to cure this inner blindness.

Look how this theme works out in the story you have just heard. The Pharisees had not been present to see for themselves that Jesus had done this great wonder. So they had the formerly blind man brought in . . . for questioning. It never occurs to the Pharisees that Jesus is the Christ, that he did this gracious act. They are 100 per cent on the other side; they immediately believe it is a trick of some kind. They really do not want to discover by questioning the man what really happened. They want to discredit Jesus and discredit the newly seeing blind man, and toward that end they set up public hearings. In that special way that authorities have, they say, "Now, son, what really happened? You can trust us." And when the man sticks to his story, they come out with their theory: that it never happened at all. This man before them really is still blind and is only pretending to see. It is a trick by this evil man Jesus.

There is the pattern, set out in its precise formal analytical lines. Jesus was powerless before this kind of inner spiritual blindness displayed by the religious authorities. They already had determined that he was a fake, a bad man, a menace to society, so they saw everything he did as further proof of *his* danger. The more he did by way of mercy and truth, the more they believed that he had to be destroyed. The only thing *he* could do that would impress them favorably would be get out of town, get lost, get killed. I submit: this is spiritual blindness; and I submit: this is spiritual blindness that cannot be cured. By Jesus, his church, or anyone.

We have lately been talking a lot in this country about racism. White racism, to be exact. The Kerner Commission report has provoked a good bit of the talk with its assertion that white racism has produced the present urban-racial crisis. Well, consider white racism as a species of this spiritual blindness for a moment. The leading characteristic of white racism is that it cannot and will not recognize itself. It cannot "see" that it cannot see. If white racism could see that it was white racism it would no longer be racist. But the nature of white racism is that it does not recognize itself to be racist. So every attempt to introduce the subject is repudiated and deepens the racism. Now it is the great wisdom of the New Testament—and I am commending this wisdom to you today—it is the great wisdom of the New Testament that spiritual blindness cannot be cured. Thus I greet with some dismay a task I have: to go out to La Grange this afternoon to talk about the urban-racial crisis as a part of a total Presbyterian effort going on in four suburban churches, simultaneously. Some people apparently still believe that those who have covered their eyes are going to be enabled to see. The deeper wisdom of the New Testament is that they are not going to see because they have their hands over their eyes.

Spiritual blindness will not be cured; in fact, will go to extraordinary lengths to defend itself against cure. This really comes out in the New Testament story.

Remember, the authorities are having a hearing. The no-longer-blind man has told them what happened, which they turn into an attack on Jesus. Now they call the parents of the no-longer-blind man in order to drug them with the threats of their very office into saying that the no-longer-blind man, their son, has never really been blind. The authorities almost succeed. These parents come as close to saying the required nothing as they can. They are frightened of the authorities. They are little people. Peasants. Many things, *bad* things, can happen to them. the authorities want to know. But the parents have al-power—against plunder, against soldiers in the night, against sudden incarceration. They tremble before the mighty authorities. They equivocate. They say, "Yes, he was blind when he was born," and, "Yes, he can see now." "How?" the authorities want to know. But the parents have already perhaps gone too far. They do not say any more.

Realistic. And outrageous. That truth should be contorted into prearranged shapes. But that, nonetheless, is the contention of this Christian writer. The authorities are not interested in the truth. They do not have an open mind for truth. They already know the truth and seek to bully evidence into confirmation. I have had occasion to observe this at close range many times since coming here almost three years ago. I have watched the poor in court. I have watched them try to tell the truth, try to tell what really happened, and find that the authorities do not want that kind of truth. I have watched poor people equivocate before the court because they surmised what the court wanted to hear and, at great detriment often to their friends or neighbors, or brothers or sisters, have said as close to nothing as possible. I have watched poor people, too, say exactly what the court wanted to hear. They say it so eagerly, hoping thereby for some favor, hoping that the authorities are noticing and are planning some great bonus for them, even if in saying what the court wants to hear they condemn one of their fellows to death or to lifelong imprisonment. And for the strange reason that the authorities need the truth beaten and twisted into certain shapes. Spiritual blindness will not be cured and will go to extraordinary lengths in order to defend itself.

Spiritual blindness can be found almost anywhere. It is not located exclusively in the authorities. But it is most dangerous there, which is why so much New Testament attention is given to the spiritual blindness of the authorities, with only incidental attention to the spiritual blindness of peasants or teachers or sailors or shortstops. Authorities who are spiritually blind in defending themselves against cure build cruel systems and crushing structures. They run civilization, in fact. They rule the world. They are the men principally responsible for the pain and heartache in the world. For all the perishing that the world does. These Christian writers refuse to have anything to do with the authorities, with government, with the Roman army, with authorized religion, with the courts, with anything authorized, because they then become authorized and fall within their power and thralldom, which is the kingdom of death. So when the writer of the Fourth Gospel pictures spiritual blindness, he necessarily talks about the authorities. In another place he writes, "God so loved the world that he gave his only Son, that whoever believes in him should not perish but have eternal life." Do you think this designation "world" applies to the mighty Roman empire only? To the generals, governors, merchants, priests, temple officials? No, it applies to the people who are perishing because of this crushing tyranny and for whom God has such love that he sends his son in order to rescue them. Jesus risks the wrath of the authorities and the death they will inflict *surely* in order to rescue the people from their perishing. Please see where Jesus comes out when it comes to rescuing a man from permanent blindness or protecting himself. He rescues the blind man. He considers life more important than the wrath of the authorities.

I am talking as though wrath were inevitable, as though the authorities were fixed in their tyrannous ways. I am talking this way because that is the way the New Testament talks. When another Christian writer says, "Be *in* the world but not of the world," he warns Christians against participating in the manufacture of death, in the wrecking of life, in callous disregard for life: which is the hallmark of the world, run as it is by the authorities. Be *in* the world on the side and at the place of the perishing, doing the work of rescue, but not *ever* under any conditions on the side of the wreckers of life, the authorities.

Now just look at this story. A grown man, born blind, blind all his days, suddenly—magnificently—is given sight, as though he had new eyes and in a very real sense *new life*. So that he no longer is captive to sightlessness, must no longer depend on others for directions, for sustenance, but now has it in himself. Free at last, you might almost say. Here we see the wish and the Christ, the rescue operation among the people; we see the basic thrust: toward full human life that cannot be gotten at by any authorities, by any tyrants, a spiritual life with new and unconditional freedom to live, which is what I take eternal life to be. This is essentially the work of the prophet standing among and for the abused against the abusers. The prophet standing against priest, general, king. The blind see! Indeed yes, and the first thing they see is their broken chains.

The lame walk! Indeed, run. Prisoners freed! Yes. The work of the Christ in rescuing the perishing for new life is a bold wish that has convulsive consequences.

There was no jubilation that the blind beggar could see *in his own home town*. There was an investigation, a hearing, an inquiry by authorities. The people who otherwise in a different life might have been having a party were reduced to whispering in the quiet of the night about the great thing that had happened, perhaps taking courage and in their hearts taking hope that finally the man God had promised to send had come.

This is not to say that Jesus was a revolutionary, an anarchist, or anything remotely like that, merely because he went to the people with mercy and strength and occasioned thereby the reflexive ugliness of the authorities. The New Testament view steers away from revolution or anarchism because it can envision no set of authorities which will not, after the revolution, begin to reduplicate the same conditions which brought on the revolution. The

Christian vision looks beyond that with perfect clarity to the one kingdom that is incorruptible, ruled by God himself. Thus do we find New Testament Christians, at any rate, in full noncooperation with the authorities. Refusing official religion, refusing to serve in the army, maintaining open alliance to their delivering God and his kingdom. They plotted no overthrow of any government; they fell into no obsequious adoration of any law and order either. They were the blind who had been given sight, which is to say, new and incorruptible life; another way of saying *eternal life*. Thus they were casual about the world and its authorities and its persecutions and its blindness.

Those are almost unbearably hard words. This casualness is what is so hard. Casualness to the world: to success, progress, reputation; casualness to the ego and to the ego ideal. Yes, and casualness to money and the things it can buy. Paul says, "I die *every day* and am risen again." That, I think, is about as casual as you can get.

But hard only in front of the authorities and their powers. With their smart questions, their raids, their insinuations, their lies.

Not hard in front of God. Freeing, gloriously releasing, to stand before God, delivering and merciful, is to have been given sight. That means: to live eternally truly, fully, freely. Amen.

22

MERCY

JONAH 1:1 to 4:11

Go and preach to . . . Cicero. What prophet wants to hear that? To a conference in the Loop, maybe, or to people who might march on Cicero again, maybe, but to Cicero? Never. It is not the danger, you see, it is the principle. A prophet does not even go to the horse racing because it is in Cicero. He wipes Cicero off his map. It is beneath him even to be upset with Cicero. Go and preach to Cicero, says God to Jonah. So Jonah goes to . . . Detroit, or he starts out for Detroit and he is detained on the way by a stupendous gale on Lake Michigan and is swallowed by a huge fish. Notice *not a whale*. A whale could swallow Jonah, all right, but no fish could, except a fish that God had designed especially to swallow Jonah and get him back to Cicero. This is a special fish not only in its size, which is enormous—maybe a large-mouthed bass that weighs about 1,540 pounds—but in its inside equipment designed with cunning oxygen facilities for passengers—just like airplanes, you see (and we don't think that is fantastic)—and food for the passengers who are going to be on board for any length of time. At the right time, when the fish has got back to shore, God tells the fish to unload its passengers, and here comes Jonah struggling up the beach at Jackson Park, wet, slimy, and very glad to be alive, although he is not sure he is dead or alive until the lifeguard at Jackson Park beach tells him not to swim out so far and if he does again he will call the you-know-who.

Now Jonah is up on the beach and God gives the command again: Go preach to *Cicero*. Detroit is not on the way to Cicero. Go to Cicero. Jonah is by now convinced. So he goes to Cicero and preaches a specific message. "You people repent thoroughly or God will wipe you out in forty days." Jonah did not like the idea of giving them even forty days. He did not like Ciceronians, period. It is a terrible place full of terrible people who are never going to understand anything. He delivers his message to the council, mayor, police, newspaper, steel mills, the crowds at the race track, and the boys in the back room, too. He leaves, confident now that he is caught up in his work, that forty days later, which will be about Bud Billikin's Day or some good day like that, Cicero will be leveled. But—amazing thing—the people in Cicero believe him. They spoil his plan. The mayor and council and officials are fearful that God will wipe them out, so they repent. They have a day of public fasting and they wear sackcloth and ashes; they shave their heads; even the race horses fast and are shaved as a sign of repentance. Does that burn Jonah up! This is what he didn't like about the project all along. God will somehow find a way to be gracious and loving to those prejudiced, mean, segregating, brick-throwing people. God will somehow come up with mercy. So Jonah wants to die of mortification that he has had anything to do with such proceedings, and he goes off west of Cicero to see how things are going to work out.

While he is thus sitting, and it was plenty hot and he is beginning to complain of maybe sunstroke, a plant begins to grow rapidly right up as he is watching until it is between him and the sun. So he has shade. Jonah is delighted with that quick-growing kind of gourd plant— at any rate it has broad leaves and is growing what looks like a gourd on it. During the night, however, God sends a cutter worm to chase the roots of the gourd plant. Next morning is hot as blazes and Jonah is very glad of that plant until he notices that, as the sun gets higher, the plant begins to wilt and die on him. On top of that there is this hot, hot wind. Everything now is wrong. God asks Jonah what is the matter and why is he looking so—well, hostile. Jonah tells God about the plant, and God tells Jonah about life. "You are concerned with this plant. You pity this plant which you didn't plant or water or make grow. It sprang up in the night and perished in the night. Should I not be concerned for Cicero, should I not *pity* Cicero, a city with 120,000 persons who can not tell between their right and left hand, and also many race horses?"

And that is the end of the story.

Herman Melville made a psychotheological thriller out of the Jonah story in *Moby Dick* through the medium of Father Mapples's sermon. Father Mapples addresses himself to Jonah's disobedience. Jonah refused to go to Nineveh and then was caught in a three-day symbolic death as the result of his disobedience. After which God recommissioned him with his prophetic task to go to Nineveh. Father Mapples thought of the fish as a whale, by the way, for reasons of relevance. The local residents were whalers.

Well, this fastening on the guilt of Jonah is magnificent Melville but very poor Old Testament. The accents of this story do not fall on Jonah's disobedience. Jonah was not disobedient as much as God was determined. The idea seems to be that Jonah was on the ship, steaming full tilt for the Straits of Gibraltar, when he should have been going up the coast only a few miles. So God used ingenuity. He made a huge gale and the sailors threw Jonah off the ship and God had this big fish handy to carry him back to land because Jonah had to go *inland*. Nineveh is like 100 miles as the arrow shoots from the coast. The fish got Jonah to the coast. That was the object and what was God's determination? To do good to Nineveh, to non-Jews, to Gentiles, to the people in black hats, to . . . enemies! Jonah incarnates popular Judaism in himself. He believes God should reserve all his energies and all his graciousness for Jews and not waste any on Gentiles. Instead, God should store up punishment and destruction for the Gentiles. He should go out of his way to be mean to Gentiles. Kill enemies. Give them boils. Stop the rain. Give their pitchers sore arms. Make their flocks barren. But against the grain of popular Judaism, God displayed his determination to do good to non-Jews.

So while we are smiling along at this delightful story, how naïve, once-upon-a-time-ish, we are getting more and more involved in an extremely serious story, ominous in a way and decisive for faith. God had pity on the great city of Nineveh, which was eight miles around; 120,000 residents, all told; pagan. These people did not know right from left. Why? Because there were his creatures in Nineveh, to say nothing of cattle creatures. They needed mercy. They needed to know specific acts of mercy. They needed to know that they had God all wrong, and no Jews were going to do that. No Jews would even conceive such a project. They operated as all political realists do. There is no forgiveness in politics. Never display mercy unless it has a clearly calculated advantage. They could not conceive such a project, these Jews to whom so much mercy had been shown, who were the very heirs of the grace of life itself. God had to lead the way.

The writer of Jonah is the most powerful voice during the time between the resettlement of Jerusalem and the coming of Jesus. He sought to return Israel *directly* to the older faith and to the determination of God to display his loving concern, through Israel, to all the peoples of the world. Not until Jesus do we hear again the cadence of loving the enemy, of healing the leper, of welcoming the prodigal, of perceiving the grace of God as immediately related to humankind and not the Jews exclusively. So just because the story is so naïve, so transparent, it carries a greater weight. A weight we must now bear among ourselves. For the message is to the new Israel, to the church, quite as fully as it was to post-exile Israel.

We are asked here to be open to such a possibility that God will be merciful to peoples we are sure do not deserve mercy and should not have it at all. I was not just funning around when I said Cicero. Cicero is as surely symbolic to us as the bastion of frightened white power, of the backlash, as Nineveh was at one time symbolic of great and dangerous military destruction to Israel. So I put the matter as fantastically as did the writer of Jonah and in that act, of course, intend to include that multitude of less symbolic, more crystallized, immediate foes, who are hostile to us personally or to us as a church. Our enemies. Or at least those we perceive as enemies. Axiomatically they are placed hereby within the orbit of our concern and are hereby designates for mercy. I realize this is nonsense. I realize that in a conflicted situation, polarized into good guys and bad guys, in such situations when we are inevitably the good guys and as such have divine favor and we know *our* cause will prevail, in such situations it is impossible to consider mercy. Mercy has no tactical usefulness. Can you imagine General Nasser explaining to Kosygin that he is going to seek an accord with the Israeli ambassador to the United Nations? Or that the Israeli government would somehow withdraw itself to pre-blitzkrieg (if you will pardon the expression) national boundaries, as an act of mercy to fellow nations within the family of nations? I at least cannot imagine it. Any more than I can imagine a rash of forgiveness breaking out among United States, North, and South Vietnamese combatants. I read in the papers this week where two elderly neighbors here in Chicago, retired now, have had this long, long flap about a flower bed right on the property line. The fuss got so hot this week that they broke out their guns and started shooting at each other. Sure.

In all such hostile situations, it is impossible to display mercy even though the merciful act might obtain mercy. Israel saw it that way. So does the church. So do we. And yet in remarkably clear ways, we are bidden to perform deeds which are sheerly impossible. Sheerly outside of history. Sheerly uncalculated. This requires something more than psychological maturity. This requires what the Bible regularly calls strength. This requires a vision. This requires being absolutely nonchalant about everything but mercy. If God should say, "Go to Cicero," we do not even raise our eyebrows, we do not consult schedules for Detroit, we go to Cicero and decide that God is the expert in justice.

Who knows? Maybe then Cicero would get itself in pretty good shape instead of being an armed hostile camp, spoiling for a fight. So beware of especially friendly 1,540-pound fish with big mouths, and hold yourselves ready for what may be a "Go-in" at any time. Amen.

23

NARROW

Psalm 2   Luke 13:22–35

Any time Jesus talks about the kingdom of God he means the kingship or "rule," the "reign" of God. Obviously, I should think, he does not believe that God had somehow and at some time stopped being the mighty and Creator King of the universe. Obviously God sustains the universe he has created; he is the Lord of all the nations and shapes people's destinies. Obviously he cares for the raven; he orders the paths of rivers; he dispatches clouds across the heavens. That is not the Kingship of God Jesus was announcing. He announced the coming of God as a master of a New Life, the inauguration of a vast renovation and restoration program. And he invited men to join him in the announcement of and participation in this new era of God's kingly dealings with men. More than casually he referred to the activity of God as "saving" activity. So much, in fact, that his followers later came to call him Savior, Rescuer, Deliverer, Restorer, as a testimony to the kingship or Rule of God over his new creation.

No person alive or who has ever lived can fail to be shaken by the power of this pronouncement of a new beginning, which is to say, a fresh start. No person alive has not courted the possibility that death itself constitutes

229

the new beginning and has looked beyond death into an afterlife and sought there his true desire: namely, the removal of suffering, the banishment of evil, reuniting with those from whom in this life he has been tragically sundered. Beneath all belief in immortality pulses the active desire for a new beginning. The sort that Nicodemus inquired of, the kind every hearer of Jesus longed for. And though we modern, socially conscious Christians are very antagonistic to the *status quo*, and rightly so, for it is harmful and the protector of evil, we are not too serious about it. Show me a successful or an unsuccessful man, show me a contented or a discontented woman, show me a youth or even a child, and I will show you a human being who regularly throws up his inner arms in disgust and wishes—desires—to chuck it all and start again somewhere else. This is the very stuff of fantasy. Here is the cauldron from which our illusions curl up so disarmingly real. On the surface the so-called *status quo* looks most invincible. But underneath in the hearts of people we see that it is held together with Scotch tape, safety pins, and paper paste.

It has been wrongly felt that this desire of the heart is a form of escapism, a reaction to the hardness of life— that is, a retreat from difficulty. But do not be misled by such brave talk. This desire is not a desire to take up beachcombing or to leave the hardness of life; it is a deeper desire than that: it is like, exactly like, the desire for immortality, only more immediate. It is the expression of the heart for a new beginning . . . now.

This is what wells up on mention of God's renovation of mankind. "*I* want some renovation." "*I* want some of that peace and blessedness, that absence of strife, some of that reconciliation. *Now*." Of course.

And Jesus says to all who desire this renovation: "Strive to enter by the narrow door; for many, I tell you, will seek to enter and will not be able." The narrow door. Strive with all your might, crawl, scramble, claw your way through: the whole power of your being devoted to the one objective of getting through the door. In another place Jesus likened this same event as being as difficult as for a huge camel to go through the tiny eye of a needle; in another place as beneficent as finding a pearl beyond price, as miraculous as being rescued from the dead. Above the narrow door there might well be a placard that reads: LOYALTY TO THE GOD OF THE NEW CREATION. But in actuality there is no such sign because to each human being the narrow gate is something very concrete. It could also be called the narrow gate to personal integrity, or the narrow gate to self-acceptance, or the narrow gate into hope, or New Life. The point being that it is the same reality no matter what names are used to describe it.

You work for a large corporate institution, let us say: public or private, it does not matter; in high or menial position, it does not matter. The fact of your working there is a source of irritation to you. You can approve the goals of the institution but not its procedures and tactics. You see employees with long service, who have dulled their sensitiveness to the procedures and hence are themselves now dull people, *and* employees who like you *feel* that something is wrong and have no way of righting the wrongs. They, like you, merely stew in the juices of daily anger. It becomes a source of personal annoyance merely to go to work there. When people you care for and respect ask you where you work, you find it a source of shame to you to tell them. The more this goes on, the more the issue of going or staying becomes the issue on which your life literally hangs. Either you continue on and give in to your no doubt exaggerated judgments— forget them—or you move out. Perhaps you cannot even put it into words, but you have this feeling that if you do not move soon, now or tomorrow afternoon, you will die, or something that is the vital part of you will die. In this way the narrow gate to personal integrity, to psychological maturity, to genuine self-acceptance, and to New Life is marked with a placard: "Quit. Do not pass Go; do not wait until you have another job safely gathered in; do not scrutinize the issue another day, quit." So that to common sense—the crowd, the others—this unparalleled summons might for all the world look like the most foolish thing a human being could do. To you it not only looks, it is, the precious narrow gateway into your full stature as a human being, into a zone of human life where God is King. The narrow gateway seldom has sharp lines of definition. Sometimes, for many people, it is merely there, vaguely, namelessly, as a presence, as a possibility for life that remains unexplored: an exit from the inner vacuum into an inner fullness that is inexactly located somewhere.

In a brilliant long short story or short novel, Albert Camus pictures a childless couple who have been married twenty years. The wife, Janine, has this inner vacuum and knows with her instincts that there is a way into inner fullness but doesn't know where it is. Her husband was a salesman who traveled in northern Algeria. She accompanied him on a trip, and they stopped one night at a desert village, once a fortress. She went up to the ramparts of the fortress in the afternoon and was stunned by the vast dryness, the coiling coldness of the scene. As though it were summoning her, that night she awakened in the midst of sleep. She heard the call. She dressed quietly, and in the night she returned to the parapet.

Not a breath, not a sound—except at intervals the muffled crackling of stones that the cold was reducing to sand—disturbed the solitude and silence surrounding Janine. After a moment, however, it seemed to her that the sky above her was moving in a sort of slow gyration. In the vast reaches of the dry, cold night, thousands of stars were constantly appearing, and their sparkling icicles, loosened at once, began to slip gradually toward the horizon. Janine could not tear herself away from contemplating those drifting flares. She was turning with them, and the apparently stationary progress little by little identified her with the core of her being, where cold and desire were now vying with each other. Before her the stars were falling one by one and being snuffed out among the stones of the desert, and each time Janine opened a little more to the night. Breathing deeply, she forgot the cold, the dead weight of others, the craziness or stuffiness of life, the long anguish of living and dying. After so many years of mad, aimless fleeing from fear, she had come to a stop at last. At the same time, she seemed to recover her roots and the sap again rose in her body, which had ceased trembling. Her whole belly pressed against the parapet as she strained toward the moving sky; she was merely waiting for her fluttering heart to calm down and establish silence within her. The last stars of the constellations dropped their clusters a little lower on the desert horizon and became still. Then, with unbearable gentleness, the water of night began to fill Janine, drowned the cold, rose gradually from the hidden core of her being and overflowed in wave after wave, rising up even to her mouth full of moans. The next moment, the whole sky stretched out over her. . . .*

The name of the narrow gate is "God is the King." The name of the narrow gate is self-acceptance. And lest you think this matter is merely talking oneself into acceptability, I want you to attend to the sobering actuality of what is involved in self-acceptance, of how much must be faced. We do not need technical facilities of psychoanalysis to know through those thousand inklings from regions beneath regions of our personal life that most of what we are is buried, hence unknown. Nor do we need a class in mental hygiene to learn that it is unknown because

* *Albert Camus*, Exile and the Kingdom (*New York: Knopf, 1958), pp. 32–33.*

so largely unacceptable. Certainly we can consult our own memories and recollect sadly the bitter hardness and uncompromising severity of judgments we have made on others because these people—often people (we say fondly) we love—exhibit what we most despise in ourselves. What would a project in self-acceptance demand? It is unimaginably difficult, fitted as we are with self-deceit, mobilized as we are against interior no less than exterior forces. Yet the minimum basis for any acceptance, other-acceptance, reality-acceptance, is self-acceptance, which to do is to enter a new life.

I was chagrined this week at a conference when some brothers maintained vigorously and sanely that black people were going to run black education or else there wasn't going to be any education. The white fathers were angry at such an exhibition of what they disdainfully called separatism. Why were they angry? Because the black demand showed up the sorry performance of white power, and the wielders of that white power were furious to have been made to face such intense moral material. Not facing it, they missed the narrow door, which is to say, self-acceptance, and New Life. Poor education. Poor administrations locked in such brave terror.

To break through . . . that narrow gate . . . requires an effort of proportions too vast to reckon. But there it is. There is a narrow, tiny gate, the name of which is self-acceptance, integrity, interior richness, renovated mankind, God is King. Self-acceptance, you see, is not theoretical-abstract. It is actual. It is like going through a narrow gate, writhing through it, scratching, clawing, smarting with the psychological perspiration of a person's most difficult labor in all of life.

But once through: There is life, the way it is supposed to be, because blessed with personal hope and personal love, built on the hard and solid fact of having been rescued, which is to say, saved.

But notice that the scene Jesus paints is one in which the hearers have not found their way in. Who find the door closed! O terrible actuality of the closed door. O double woe in the words of the householder, "Depart from me." Name-dropping does not avail. "We saw you. We ate, we drank with you. You taught in our towns." So what? Your intentions were against entering, obviously. You lacked desire. But more, you have no sense for the seriousness of life. See how you wail and pound and scream. Exactly. A part of your infantile way. Like a child you thought the door would be always open. Sometimes doors close. The night falls. The other sheep must be protected from howling wolves.

And you look in on the feast. Abraham, Isaac, Jacob, the prophets—men—strange men from east, west, north, and south. Gathered here in great good cheer. A roaring fire. Laughing. And you outside the closed door or the narrow gate. That it was narrow does not matter. Now you would gladly renounce all to enter. Now you would count being inside more important than clothes, bank account, reputation, mother, father, religion, suffering—even death. But the door is closed and you did not in fact count the New Life more important than anything else.

So weeping and gnashing teeth. Recall the question asked of Jesus, "Lord, will those who are saved be few?" Few?

"Will those who are saved be few?" What a question. As though life were a numbers game, a statistical series. The question is not manyness or fewness. The question, while there is yet time, is: Strive to enter the narrow door, if indeed that is the great and only desire of heart. Amen.

24

STONES

LUKE 19:29–40

Even when Alfred Hitchcock is off form, he generally makes better movies than any other American producer-director, including William Wyler, Robert Rossen, John Frankenheimer, and Fred Coe. I refer specifically to one of the movies Hitchcock made which was not really his best, the movie called "The Birds," a movie none of the named producer-directors would have attempted. This movie, as you may recall, tells the story of a bird revolution against human exploitation. Normally you think of birds as being timid, inoffensive types. Their only means of attack are beaks and claws. But there are more birds with these puny attacking devices than you realize. A lot more. One bird or a dozen birds attacking a human being wouldn't really present a big problem. But six hundred birds would. Especially if the birds were angry and persistent, filled with the reckless all-outness of true revolutionaries. In this movie not hundreds but thousands upon thousands of birds make direct and near-successful attacks upon the humanity in a town north of San Francisco and its institutions. Hitchcock goes out of his way to show that birds can kill people, destroy their boats, automobiles, and houses. And Hitchcock does not exclude some nice

236

birds, such as canaries or doves. All birds, all types of birds, all sizes and colors of birds are in revolt. Throwing off their cages, as it were, and going after this shotgun-toting—shotgun-shooting—bunch. Sure it is unbelievable. It is unbelievable until you see it, until you see birds go right through a house, an ordinary house protected only against wind, sun, rain, and burglars. Then you may still not believe birds capable of this level of violent destructiveness, but you do not believe it casually. You do not go away from the theater thinking that Hitchcock has once more pulled your leg, ha-ha. You leave the theater on the look-out for any noticeable concentration of birds: a believing nonbeliever.

For our purposes this morning, with a text in which Jesus said that if his disciples did not ecstatically shout when he entered Jerusalem the stones themselves would cry out . . . yes . . . confronted with shouting stones, it is well that we allow Mr. Hitchcock to restore us to our proper senses about the enormous creaturely power of—well, stones and birds, of winds and oceans. We who live in cities especially, in contrived exclusion from contact with these creaturely powers, we must be returned to our proper senses and that best by recalling what a large continent on what a huge globe Chicago is located. In these cities we tend to think of natural creatures in terms of Jackson Park or the Dan Ryan Forest Preserve or the occasional farm that school children may briefly visit . . . or a zoo. It then becomes a short step from this truncated experience of natural beauty and power to the assumption that all nature is like Jackson Park or the Brookfield Zoo, safely under the dominion (like everything else) of the Cook County Democratic Committee and its chairman, Richard J. Daley.

In this sense, then, Alfred Hitchcock's movie is very helpful to us Christians this morning because he presents a picture of nature in revolt, escaping this absolute human dominion, rejecting always being shot and caged and poisoned in favor of violent revolutionary activity. As though, you see, human beings permitted birds to exist and could withdraw that permission at any time. As though human beings took no proper thought for their fellow creatures, the birds. This movie, I say, is very helpful to us Christians this morning as we try to understand the possibility and meaning of the stones crying out. Because stones also, like trees and flowers and grass and the mountains on which stones are located, are creatures as human beings are, which have their proper place in the entire creation and which have specific functions and live under definite mandates and are, too, accountable to the Creator. Yes, stones, lizards, and moss. Yes, snakes and mice. Yes, cougars, mustangs, and impalas. All in the coherence of created order, all given tasks, power to exist, from whom obedience is required as surely as it is from the most spectacular beings on earth, namely us . . . human beings. So that if the Messianic Deliverer, Jesus, entering the city of his father David in order, precisely, to deliver that city, save it from its religious idiocy, is not greeted for what he truly is by the *human* beings on the scene, then that does not exhaust the beings present, some of whom—the stones, let us say—*will* act in the place of the disobedient humans and cry out with joy for the coming of the mighty King Jesus. The stones along the wayside and on the curbs—no, the curbs themselves—and the stones in the walls of buildings and the wall surrounding the city crying out, bursting their inorganic muteness in testimony to the coming of the King Jesus. Shouting stones, bursting-into-activity stones, toppling the buildings of which they had been made part. Crying-out stones, acting as proxy human beings under direct command from their

Creator as creatures welcoming the presence of the Delivering One, the Mighty One.

This verse provides great comfort to Christian people. This verse retrains our attention to the vastness of the program of deliverance God has initiated and reminds us that God is prepared to act beyond us and in ways both frightening and surprising if we falter and too much yield as Christian people to the temptations of folly and irrelevance. Ah, yes. Here is the comfort. Justice, for instance, is not a moment-by-moment achievement first reverenced, then denied, or an idea inside the heads of people who can also then get it into their heads to reverence totalitarian politics and policies of apartheid and racial genocide. Justice abides in the structure of creation itself and is thus as old and enduring as the oceans and mountains. If humankind falters in heeding its demands, justice will recall the creation into significantly different arrangements. Were the stones to conspire this moment against *us* . . . look around. Look at all those stones. Big stones. We are outnumbered and without defense. Stones shouting for the justice, acting in behalf of the justice we have compromised beyond further repair. And if the Justice Department cannot somehow protect the voters of Gary from the provocative presence of the National Guard and the Lake County Election Board, and as a consequence Richard Hatcher is cut down, so that democracy in one more instance is denied in this land of the free, then, my friends, do not believe that you will be alone in your wrath. Do not at all costs go away from that event sure that there is no such thing as justice. The offense will be not only against Richard Hatcher and the people he so brilliantly represents but against the creation itself and all of its realms and orders, its species and its spheres. The lake and the buildings and the streets of Gary will observe, whether

we turn our eyes or not, and with far more deeply structured and inalterable commitment to justice than fickle,
self-serving, personal-justice-seeking human beings. Here
is the comfort: that the great stone, which in obedience
to God conspired in Jesus's resurrection and stepped aside
for its master, and the mountains, which in the ecstatic
language of the Psalmist dance and clap their hands, por-
tray the bottomless determination of God to have on this
earth peace among men. We somehow think of ourselves
as having originated the idea. In our plunging furiously
into the fray, we act as though the entire battle for peace
and justice will be lost if we falter. Silly Christian people
who should know better. I do not fault the passion, the
numberless hours, the determination. Quite the opposite:
I admire and am thrilled by it. But please add perspective
and Christian learning to your intensity. Please be reminded
of your colleagues in this human business, the whole created order, all the creatures of God who desire even more
than you the day when the love Jesus announced and enacted reigns throughout the earth. And please be reminded
that God is not only resourceful and responsive in dealing with human recalcitrance. He also plans ahead. He
ordains. He fashions the structures in which vaunted freedom operates. Above all, and for your comfort, be mind-
ful that God is the Creator omnipotent whose ways do
not change.

Now does this seem like a pretty romantic idea of
nature? Back to good old Jean Jacques Rousseau? Hah.
Am I saying that when all other friends fail you you still
have your friends the rocks and the sky? No. Nothing
of the sort. I have not gone soft in the head (I don't
think). I am trying to prepare you in advance for the
possible cataclysms the human race faces. The disorders.
The agony. Not merely the human race in general but
the human race right around here in Chicago. I want to

comfort you with the certainty that there are structures of mercy, rightness-reaching measures, in this universe which are deeper, more resourceful, more powerful than man's most stubborn bigotry. I want to prepare you for the response of the creation to the racist madness we practice here in America and in Vietnam. This is the disorder and it will be healed by new order, and as old law remains the domain of cynical politicians there shall be new law, and new people, even if that requires the toppling of civilization itself. That is what is buried in this apparently casual remark of Jesus: that the stones would cry out were the disciples to have remained silent. Comfort. Comfort? Spread the tokens of your *gladness* upon this table. Speak peace and love to one another. Repeat to one another the promises of God: that the lame will walk; the imprisoned go free; the blind see; the leper be cleansed; the deprived be enriched; the low made high; all people united; the hungry fed; the naked clothed: all men brothers, coming from east and west, from north and south, to congregate in the rich loving life which knows God as King. Rejoice and be glad. The disorders that we shall all surely endure will be the occasion for Christian people the more to praise God, and if we fail now or then, you may be assured, the very stones will cry out. Amen.

25

PERISHING

I Kings 17:1–24

All of the neighboring countries around Israel, and throughout the Near East, had kings who were regarded as gods and who returned this regard by believing themselves to be gods. They weren't religious fanatics. That isn't the point. They were tyrants. Even the great kings for whom national advantage in the pressure cooker of Mediterranean politics was placed ahead of personal advantage were tyrants, and most of them were not great kings. They just looked great with their gold pants and 1,000 personal policemen and 5,000 personal slaves and 100 wives and these great wine cellars and private Boeing 720s all their own to go to Cannes and Acapulco and Rio. But tyrants. So were the kings of Israel during the ninth century B.C., during the time of Elijah, during the times that our Old Testament lection tells about. I say kings. Plural. There were two kings in Israel. One was Ahab, and he was bad enough all by himself. The other was Jezebel, his wife, whom he married for political and commercial reasons because she was the daughter of a neighboring tyrant over in Damascus. And Jezebel was something else. Jezebel was Barbara Hutton, Rita Hayworth, Lurleen Wallace, and Madylyn Murray all put together. Rich, tempestuous, cun-

242

ning, jet-set-oriented, bigoted, and strong. Ahab was no match for her, and by himself Ahab was bad enough. So the two of them really were messing up Israel.

The prophet Elijah, without any fanfare, any build-up, just appears on the scene and begins a revolution to unseat these kings. Let us be more accurate in our use of language. Elijah just appeared on the scene and announced that God was going to unseat Ahab and Jezebel and any king that might follow them. God had a controversy with these kings. No king can act like gods in Israel. No tyrants allowed. Elijah and his successor Elisha did it, too. They hatched a popular revolution and an entirely new figure swept into the kingship of Israel, a fellow named Jehu. Now you can imagine how popular Elijah was at the royal palace. Here he was storming up and down Israel preaching revolution, outlining the issues, establishing the nature of God's controversy with the kings, and because he was a prophet he had to be treated like the sacred cows in India. You don't dare knock them in the head. You just have to let them go wherever they fancy going.

The kings were furious—double-triple furious, apoplectic—when Elijah announced that there would be a three-year drought. Think of that. No rain, not even any dew, for three whole years. Well, they were supposed to be gods on the earth, you see. The heavenly gods they worshiped *in* Israel, the Baals—well, they were supposed to be the very gods who were good at rainfall, fertility of crops and flocks. So when Elijah announces no rain for three years he is not being mean, trying to starve the people out. And it is not because he doesn't like farms or doesn't want the farm vote. Elijah is declaring that Yahweh is the Lord of Israel. And he is the one who has created everything that is, including the clouds that bear rain in off the Mediterranean, and if God says no rain, you better start looking for deep wells because, mister, it is not going to rain. He is the real God, and let's just see what kind of fake gods are parading around Israel in their gold pants and Ferraris. Let's just see if they can drum up a little rain or even some dew. Any god ought to be able to do that. Right? Showdown.

Remember, the real issue was the insulting despotism of the kings. Their arrogance. Their running over the peasants. Their installing hot and cold running priests all over the place. Religion-in-Israel's-life campaigns every other week. Their use of the military. The inevitable plundering of peasants, of the little defenseless people in Israel. This was the real issue that was being brought to a showdown when Elijah announced that God was going to stop all rain, all dew, for three years. Not one year. That could be misunderstood. Not two. Even that could be misunderstood. It was pretty dry there, and some precedent existed for pretty long dry spells. But never three whole years without any rain, any dew.

And what happens to Elijah in these three years? He never went to seminary, so he can't go back to seminary to get his Ph.D. Probably never ever heard of Karl Barth. He can't go into the towns because he might get . . . arrested, as it were. The only place he can go is into the safety of the wilderness, and that is where he is found in the story you heard read. Being fed manna and meat by ravens—you should be able to pick that up—just like Moses and the freshly delivered Israel on its way to the promised land. Elijah also drank out of a brook. But then, without dramatic flourishes, Elijah is sent to go to a little non-Israelite village and wait out the drought there in the household and in the keeping of a widow. Our writer, capable, as you have heard, of remarkably brilliant prose effects, then tells us how Elijah obsequiously presents himself to the widow and how the widow declares herself immediately: she will go to fix bread and give water "that we may eat . . . and die," and then Elijah promises that her meal and oil supplies will not fail. Just as the mercies of God will not fail, just as the determination of God to get rid of Ahab and Jezebel will not fail. You keep watching your meal and oil, and if it runs out, *then* you will know there is no God in Israel. She is impressed, and they go on like this for an unspecified length of time.

Then a terrible crisis develops. The widow's son becomes desperately ill, at the point of death. The boy is perishing. The woman immediately blames it on Elijah. She has perhaps committed a sin, and this man of God's presence has garnered retribution and placed it on the boy. She is upset. She, in good cause-and-effect fashion, sees the boy sick, sees Elijah in her household, and puts the two together. *He* has somehow caused the boy's sickness. Now look. Before we declare the woman emotionally overwrought and move on to the healing, let's stop. This incident is similar to another series of incidents in the whole Elijah story. At one point, for instance, Ahab and Elijah choose to meet each other. Alone. Ahab says, "Is it you, you troubler of Israel?" Well, who is troubling Israel? Elijah or . . . Ahab? It all depends. From the point of the Establishment with its assumption of divine dynastic power: but of course, Elijah is the troubler, naturally. Jailed. Run out of town. Lynched. Agitator. The whole bag of standard appellations is available. Elijah is destroying the future and upsetting the present tranquility of the country. But from Elijah's position, from the standpoint of the controversy *God* was conducting with Ahab, *Ahab* had destroyed the tranquility of Israel by being a tyrant. You see? Ahab did not have to be a tyrant; he did not have to domesticate the press; he did not have to plunder the defenseless poor; he did not have to misuse the military; he did not have to put personal advantage above national interest. But he did. So *he* was the troubler of Israel. Elijah was attempting to bring tranquility back by unseating the troubler.

As you can guess, Elijah had a hard time of it. Imagine how far he got in trying to get his point out in the *Tribune,* which was helping the people to understand that *Elijah* was Israel's troubler. Well. This is the same thing going on with the widow, devout *Tribune* reader that she was. She connected Elijah and trouble. We have to read the story bigger than it is so that we can see the whole landscape of the revolution illustrated in this act of the widow in placing the blame on Elijah for the critical illness of her son. And Elijah, one of the great debaters of all times, capable of eloquence, irony, hilarity, one of the rare great talking men in all history, this Elijah does not say one word of rebuttal or explanation. He acts. He goes to the boy who is perishing. The reason and explanation are bypassed. He does not show the widow that her doctrine of causality is O.K. but her understanding of the doctrine weird. He just goes to the perishing boy, takes him to an upper room (where have you heard this before?), practices mouth-to-mouth resuscitation on the boy three times, and cries to Yahweh to let the boy's nephesh return to the boy. Yahweh hears the cry. The perishing boy is saved. He is delivered from death. In the middle of a revolution, a showdown, this hated, feared, maligned man rescues the perishing; he cares for the dying.

How about that? Whoever thinks of a prophet being able to save life? We think of prophets out there on the streets in contact with kings, entering into public controversies. We are right. That is the business of a prophet. But Elijah also saved life. It is better to save life than to have a good revolution, and now let's come to the end: the widow, the non-Israelite, trapped with everyone else in the terrible drought, sees Elijah as the man of God

246

and knows that the word of truth is in his mouth. Ladies and gentlemen, this is more than mere gratitude, more than the relief of a mother who is presented with a live boy. It is also representative of the kind of support that Elijah began to get from the little people who were being hurt more than the kings or the affluent by this protracted drought. The little people had begun to see Elijah's point. They began to fall in behind him. They saw the scene under Ahab and Jezebel as it really was. The poor were the first to be drafted, enslaved, robbed, killed, pushed around by these divine-being-type kings. So "We're with you, Elijah!"

Now I want to comment on the perishing boy and all of the realistic politics of the big-picture boys who do not perceive perishing children. Yesterday's news tells of an abandoned child in Detroit who perished. The neighbors knew about that child, but they did not want to butt in and thus showed they did not care. Just like the big wheeler-dealer fly-around-the-country specialists, so high—by which I mean, of course, so abstract—they have no idea of perishing children. They are not seen because they are not within the field of the specialist's ordinary sight. As the B-52 pilots never see the Vietnamese children who perish when the bombs explode. Whoever does see perishing Vietnamese or American children? Whoever does take a good close-up look at perishing American children in our decaying school buildings, staffed by decaying teachers, the same children who return from school to crumbling apartment buildings? Yes. Paul Goodman has looked. His cry of anguish is contained in his book, *Growing Up Absurd.* He says we raise children to perform in the economic system, and when they get there they see none of the jobs are worth doing. But they have to fit in. Adults are outraged when the now-raised children tell them that the jobs are not worth doing, because they are the same jobs

which the adults are doing right now. Observing the outrage, the now-raised children see they have two options:
to perish in our withering condemnation or to perish in
the absurd system. That is the way it goes: perish or
perish. How's that for a first-class horror?

This scripture raises a raw question with us: Can we
as a nation, or as individuals in the nation, take time out
from the big picture, from our national pursuits, from
our playing around so comfortably in the establishment
with Ahab and Jezebel, take time out from all of this
to care for our perishing children? I raise this question
with you because by your actions as a congregation you
have already demonstrated that you care for perishing
children. You already know about saving life. You have
postponed the big picture, the big deal, the messing around,
the appealing to fancy people—postponed it indefinitely,
forever if necessary—in order to care for perishing children.
Why do I raise such a question with you *of all people?*
Just because children perish one by one at times and in
places of horribly immediate circumstance. That one hundred of those four thousand children have already been
saved could easily obscure the one perishing child *today.*
Do you see? It is my hope that such a scripture will em-
bolden us always to look for that one child, even if in
looking and attending we are kept from some important
appointments with the big-picture boys in the Loop. The
great revolution can wait or will go on under its own
momentum. Never fear. Of course, in peculiar ways the
revolution can be seen for what it really is in the acts of
rescuing perishing children. What is a revolution anyway
if, in joining its fervor, children are allowed to die because
eyes cannot focus on such small objects? I call you to it,
to the infinitely important and revolutionary task of raising
strong, forthright, healthy children, in the failing of which
nothing else you might do would matter. Amen.